IF GOD DOES NOT PERMIT A WOMAN TO PREACH THEN GOD MUST BE A SEXIST

The divine revelation on the GOD-given position of the WOMEN of GOD

Minister Lamont McLaurin

Table of Contents

PREFACE

I have been preaching the gospel for over twenty-five years now. I have been preaching with authority and power. However, in the recesses of my heart there was trepidation. I knew God had called me, and I really did not want to answer the call, but the burning I felt in my soul could not be extinguished. The only time I would get relief was when I shared the gospel with power and demonstration. Yet the trepidation persisted. The trepidation had persisted because there were those who I honored and respected who told me that I was out of order.

I am presently, the only female pastor in an area with all male pastors, and they give me no respect. They meet with each other and I am not invited to the meetings. They have programs and my church is not invited. The politicians in the area go to them, but my opinion is not important to them. I shrugged these things off as if they do not bother me, but when my husband told me to get out of the pulpit or else he would leave me, I had to make a decision—and the decision was not easy. Why did I have to make this decision after nine years of pastoring and twenty-five years of ministering? Then came this teaching on a Tuesday night on June 10, 2008

Beloved, my life has never been the same, my ministry has been transformed, and any man who has a problem with me in the pulpit must see God about it. I will no longer receive the spirit of inferiority, I will no longer allow anyone to tell me who I am, and if you thought, the God in me was dynamic before, LOOK OUT. God used Bishop T.D. Jakes to loose the woman but Minister Lamont McLaurin has been used to set us free.

This book reads as if you were watching a trial and the defense attorney was defending the case of the God who called the woman to preach. The question is, Is He or is He not a sexist?

Sit back, take your time, and read this explosive biblical revelation that God has given us—line upon line, precept upon precept.

What a revelation.

Dr. Marilynn Miles

Chapter 1

The Entrance of Your WORD Gives Light

Sexist: Behavior, condition, or attitude that fosters stereotypes of social roles based on sex.

If you believe that the Bible is the infallible, inerrant Word of God, you must also believe that every word the apostle Paul spoke came directly out of God's mouth.

Galatians 1:11- 12

> *But I certify you, brethren, that the gospel which was preached of me is not after man. For I neither received it of man, neither was I taught it, but by the revelation of Jesus Christ.*

One Tuesday evening while preparing for a Bible study, one of the faithful texted me and complained to me that she was very troubled in her spirit with respect to women preaching. The week prior, she asked," how could I discern spiritual answers in the Bible?" I responded, "Read *John 16:13...*"

> *Howbeit when he, the Spirit of truth, is come, he will guide you into all truth: for he shall not speak of himself; but whatsoever he shall hear, that shall he speak: and he will show you things to come.*

She responded, "I did that, and I am still experiencing insuperable (extremely difficult time understanding) difficulties watching Paula White and Joyce Meyers and being blessed and reading **1 Timothy 2:12-13** and not being able to reconcile the two."

1 Timothy 2:12-13

> *But I suffer not a woman to teach, nor to usurp authority over the man, but to be in silence. For Adam was first formed, then Eve.*

At this time, I told her that God would give her an answer in the near future and we exchanged goodbyes.

At that time, I sat back in my study perplexed. Why was I perplexed? The reason that I was perplexed was because the very same question that burdened her heart and had her querulous was the exact question that burdened my heart only she had the boldness to come forward while I sheepishly kept the matter at heart ostensibly because my Pastor is a woman.

As time went on that week, a consortium of T.V. programs popped up either condemning women pastors, or women pastors were attempting to apologize for their positioning.

Two women that impressed my heart emotionally were Sarah Sentilles author of "The Church of Her" and Anne Fuller Lightener, the female Bishop who was denied Bishopric recently.

What was telling was both women had very precious spirits and they were in effect pleading to be accepted but did not have a solid Biblical foundation to support their positions, although they were convicted that they were being led by the Spirit.

At this time, I sat back in my study for a period of 7 days and asked God to speak to my heart, I told God that I knew that I wasn't worthy but please speak to me like He spoke to Moses not in vision and dark sayings but face-to-face.

I further told God that this topic was a hotly debated and grossly misunderstood and that I needed clarity on this issue that was fraught with ambiguity.

Psalm 119:130

¹³⁰The entrance of thy words giveth light; it giveth understanding unto the simple.

For years, Apostle Paul persecuted the church in ignorance. Although he was a Hebrew of Hebrews, taught scripture by Gamaliel a Pharisee of Pharisees who was a celebrated doctor of the law, Saul affluent in Greek with a Roman Citizenship, still he persecuted the church, but he did it in ignorance.

Much like opponents of women preaching Saul interpreted scripture literally and actually thought, that he was doing God a service. It was not until he received the Holy Spirit did he convert, repent and see the **Light**.

Paul's heart was so hardened toward Christians that it took Stephen's execution to allow Christ to penetrate Saul's heart.

Acts 7:54-60

⁵⁴When they heard these things, they were cut to the heart, and they gnashed on him with their teeth.

11

[55]But he, being full of the Holy Ghost, looked up steadfastly into heaven, and saw the glory of God, and Jesus standing on the right hand of God,

[56]And said, Behold, I see the heavens opened, and the Son of man standing on the right hand of God.

[57]Then they cried out with a loud voice, and stopped their ears, and ran upon him with one accord,

[58]And cast him out of the city, and stoned him: and the witnesses laid down their clothes at a young man's feet, whose name was Saul.

[59]And they stoned Stephen, calling upon God, and saying, Lord Jesus, receive my spirit.

[60]And he kneeled down, and cried with a loud voice, Lord, lay not this sin to their charge. And when he had said this, he fell asleep.

Acts 8:1

[1]And Saul was consenting unto his death. And at that time there was a great persecution against the church which was at Jerusalem; and they were all scattered abroad throughout the regions of Judaea and Samaria, except the apostles.

Acts 9:1-6

[1]And Saul, yet breathing out threatenings and slaughter against the disciples of the Lord, went unto the high priest,

[2]And desired of him letters to Damascus to the synagogues, that if he found any of this way, whether they were men or women, he might bring them bound unto Jerusalem.

> *³And as he journeyed, he came near Damascus: and suddenly there shined round about him a light from heaven:*
>
> *⁴And he fell to the earth, and heard a voice saying unto him, Saul, Saul, why persecutest thou me?*
>
> *⁵And he said, Who art thou, Lord? And the Lord said, I am Jesus whom thou persecutest: it is hard for thee to kick against the pricks.*
>
> *⁶And he trembling and astonished said, Lord, what wilt thou have me to do? And the Lord said unto him, Arise, and go into the city, and it shall be told thee what thou must do.*

You see it took a devout man like Steven, to not only give his life, but to pray for Saul and the Jews while they were opening his head with 50 lb. stones.

These words "Lord lay not this sin to their charge" had Saul in deep meditation. So deep that it allowed THE **LIGHT** OF THE WORLD TO PENETRATE HIS HEART and convert him when Saul was on the road to Damascus no doubt was he thinking about Stephen's murder and Christ took that opportunity to fulfill his WORD in

Isaiah 42:6

> *⁶I the LORD have called thee in righteousness, and will hold thine hand, and will keep thee, and give thee for a covenant of the people, for a light of the Gentiles;*

Acts 13:47

> *⁴⁷For so hath the Lord commanded us, saying, I have set thee to be a light of the Gentiles, that*

thou shouldest be for salvation unto the ends of the earth.

As you see once the **Light** penetrated Saul's heart not only did his name change, his entire life changed. The very office that he persecuted (Christianity) he became an Apostle for and later gave his life for because once the Spirit of the word entered his heart it gave **Light**. It illuminated the word so Paul could understand what God meant by the word and not discern it according to the flesh. Additionally it allowed God to reveal 2/3rds of the New Testament through this earthen vessel.

Now how does Paul's experience dovetail with the context of this book? Well from the onset of the interchange, it was mentioned that two women of God were found distraught and disturbed on nationwide T.V. with respects to their acceptance in the pulpit or put in another way their rejection from their brethren in the pulpit.

Scripture says in Romans 14:17

[17]For the kingdom of God is not meat and drink; but righteousness, and peace, and joy in the Holy Ghost.

Clearly these women were not experiencing what scripture has promised, due to the consistent outpouring of ostracism, criticism, rejection and the like because the word never entered the heart of opponents of women preaching therefore they are in darkness still and can only respond with the fruit of darkness. Underscored below are the fruit.

Galatians 5:19

[19]Now the works of the flesh are manifest, which are these; Adultery, fornication, uncleanness, lasciviousness,

Now the works of the flesh are clear

1) Envy
2) Strife
3) Contentions
4) Dissentions
5) Selfish Ambitions
6) Jealousies

As you see because of the lack of light and discerning by the letter and not manifested and the word never get to enter the believer's heart with the special revelation that women are in correct Biblical standing when they preach.

Let us test this theory by reasserting the scripture in 1st Timothy 2:12 and 1st Corinthians 14:34-35 let's do some make shift scripture juggling.

1st Timothy 2:12

[12]But I suffer not a woman to teach, nor to usurp authority over the man, but to be in silence.

1st Corinthians 14:34-35

[34]Let your women keep silence in the churches: for it is not permitted unto them to speak; but they are commanded to be under obedience as also saith the law.

> *[35]And if they will learn any thing, let them ask their husbands at home: for it is a shame for women to speak in the church.*

Wow!!! How Blind

Let your people of color keep silent in the churches, for it is shameful for them to speak in churches, let the dark man learn in silence. *Gender Same as Skin Color ???*

If the infallible, inerrant word of God read like that, there would not be Black clergy, moreover, there would be a thin thread of minorities in Christendom and God would be ostracized as a 24 carat racist.

But when scriptures reads the literal interpretation about women, opponents of women preaching uncritically swallow the literal tense whole, capriciously ignoring what the Spirit is actually saying to the believer, and never indict Paul or God as being a sexist. Let us examine this test in truth.

Where people of color or minorities would have taken offense to this, specifically having insuperable difficulty understanding how could a Holy, Loving God espouse this apparently racist doctrine to mankind and more than likely rejecting the doctrine, women have, and I say this with tremendous reverence and respect have held their peace throughout all of the gainsaying, criticism, rejection and the like.

Finally, a book has been revealed that gives women a **BIBLICAL BASIS** for their reason of hope.

A little arrogant too

WARNING

The upcoming chapters of this book will present three distinct cataclysms that may have a shocking effect on your philosophical outlook on women shepherding. These cataclysms will:

1) Rock the world's theology and ideology with respect to women in the pulpit.
2) Unveil thousands of years of power, wisdom, and position suppressed by sexism.
3) Women of all faiths and walks of life will prosper socially, economically, politically, positionally, and relationally if they receive this revelation.

God only sanctions one faith !!!

Chapter 2

MY PEOPLE ARE DESTROYED FOR LACK OF KNOWLEDGE

Hosea 4:6

⁶My people are destroyed for lack of knowledge: because thou hast rejected knowledge, I will also reject thee, that thou shalt be no priest to me: seeing thou hast forgotten the law of thy God, I will also forget thy children.

The question—and there is no middle ground—is if Paul spoke by divine inspiration then God would clearly have to be indicted and charged with being a *sexist*. No theologian with a sober scholarship about theology would have the temerity to debate that

Sexist: Discrimination of a person based on sex.

In order for God to be a sexist, we have to examine His motivation, His ulterior motive. What would be the motive of any sexist? Answer — gender.

Does God Have a Gender?

First, the Bible aptly codifies that God created man in His own image, in the image of God He created him, male and female He created them. So clearly a reasonable person can arrive at the logical conclusion that because God created both male and female in His image, He does not participate in one gender or the other. Put another way, because God transcends gender it is anatomically impossible for Him to be a sexist.

Sexism, like racism, derived from human wisdom.

James 3:14-17

[14]But if ye have bitter envying and strife in your hearts, glory not, and lie not against the truth.
[15]This wisdom descendeth not from above, but is earthly, sensual, devilish.
[16]For where envying and strife is, there is confusion and every evil work.
[17]But the wisdom that is from above is first pure, then peaceable, gentle, and easy to be intreated, full of mercy and good fruits, without partiality, and without hypocrisy.

Scripture clearly explains that human wisdom is fleshly, sensual, and demonic.

Case in Point: Let us look at the sister of sexism, **racism.**

In the past, and in some social circles today, a spurious theory persisted that the white man was the devil and that African Americans or blacks in general derived from apes. Despite a wealth of scientific proof and spiritual enlightenment, some from these people and other races still hold fast to these destructive, demonic heresies that have been proven false Let us first examine the theory of blacks deriving from apes. If a person holds to a biblical worldview then it precludes humans deriving from anything other than God.

Genesis 1:25-26

²⁵And God made the beast of the earth after his kind, and cattle after their kind, and every thing that creepeth upon the earth after his kind: and God saw that it was good.
²⁶And God said, Let us make man in our image, after our likeness: and let them have dominion over the fish of the sea, and over the fowl of the air, and over the cattle, and over all the earth, and over every creeping thing that creepeth upon the earth.

As confirmed by science, the DNA for a fetus is not the DNA for a fish, and the DNA for a fish is not the DNA for a frog. Rather the DNA of a fetus, fish, and frog are uniquely programmed for reproduction each after its own kind; thus while the Bible does allow for microevolution (transitions within kinds), it does not allow for macroevolution (amoebas evolving into apes or apes evolving into astronauts).

To say that the white man derived from Satan physically is equally absurd and demonstratively false.

Demons are non-sexual, non-physical beings and as such are incapable of having sexual relations and producing physical offspring. To say that demons can create bodies with

DNA and fertile sperm is to say that demons have creative power, which is an exclusive divine prerogative of God.

Jesus said in **Luke 24:39**

[39]Behold my hands and my feet, that it is I myself: handle me, and see; for a spirit hath not flesh and bones, as ye see me have.

Now that we have concluded that sexism, like racism, comes from human wisdom and not from God, then why would God have Paul write the following Scripture passages, which obviously prohibit women from preaching and appear to be sexist.

If my football Coach wants me to play Defensive end instead of Defensive Line Backer what Kind of prejudice does he have??

Chapter 3

Rubber Meets the Road: The Hard Sayings of Paul

1 Corinthians 14:34-35

Let your women keep silence in churches: for it is not permitted unto them to speak, but they are commanded to be under obedience, as also saith the law. And if they learn anything, let them ask their husbands at home, for it is a shame for women to speak in the church.

1 Timothy 2:11-14

Let the woman learn in silence with all subjection.
But I suffer not a woman to teach, nor to usurp authority over the man, but to be in silence. For Adam was first formed, then Eve, and Adam was not deceived, but the woman being deceived was in the transgression.

B efore a person can receive Scripture they must have the ability to hear what the Spirit says and how to divide the Word that it harmonizes with the nature and character of God (pure, peaceable, without hypocrisy).

2 Timothy 2:15

Study to show thyself approved unto God, a workman that needeth not to be ashamed, rightly dividing the Word of Truth.

Revelation 3:22

He that hath an ear, let him hear what the Spirit saith unto the churches [people].

At first blush, when you read the aforementioned Scripture verses you have two schools of thought.

You have the sexist school, which speaks like this: When the apostle Paul was led of the Holy Spirit to give reason why a woman cannot bear authority in the church, and teach and preach to men, he pointed back to the Garden of Eden.

But I suffer [allow] not a woman to teach, nor to usurp authority over the man, but to be in silence. For Adam was first formed, then Eve, and Adam was not deceived, but the woman being deceived was in transgression.

Then you have the apologetic school, which says Paul was only attempting to correct loudmouth women who were yelling from one side of the church to the other. Both of these conclusions are silenced by careful consideration of the context.

First, Paul obviously does not intend to say that women must *always* be silent in a church or there would not be choirs, deaconesses, and female Bible study teachers; rather, in a culture in which women were largely illiterate and unlearned, Paul was saying that **until** a woman learns she must not presume to teach.

If Paul had intended to say a woman must **always** be silent, he would not have given women instructions on how to pray or prophesy publicly in church.

1 Corinthians 11:5

But every woman that prayeth or prophesieth with her head uncovered dishonoureth her head: for that is even all one as if she were shaven.

Moreover, by alluding to Eve's deception in the garden, Paul underscores how crucial it is that women, like men, involve themselves in learning. Far from chastening Eve for her role in the fall, Paul chastises the Jewish men of his day for excluding women from learning, thus leaving them vulnerable to deception.

Just as Adam was responsible for failing to protect Eve from deception, so too the men of Paul's day would be held responsible.

So when Paul alluded to Eve being deceived, he actually charged Adam with not girding her properly.

Really?? when? How?

Case in Point:

Question: Why didn't the serpent tempt Adam directly?

Answer: Because he knew that God gave Adam primary instructions and Eve received secondary instructions from Adam, and because of pride Adam didn't want Eve to be on the same footing as himself, and so he failed to gird Eve properly. The fierce proponent of the sexist doctrine that women can't preach actually mirrors Adam's personality. If you want to come to the truth of the fall, do not just judge the fall, but also judge *how* Eve fell and you will clearly see why Paul says in...

Romans 5:12-14

Wherefore, as by one **man** *sin entered into the world, and death by sin; and so death passed upon all men, for that all have sinned: (For until the law sin was in the world: but sin is not imputed when there is no law. Nevertheless, death reigned from Adam to Moses, even over them that had not sinned after the similitude of Adam's transgression, who is the figure of him that was to come.*

Chapter 4

THE FALL: (Did God Say That?)

Genesis 2:16-17

And the Lord God commanded the man, saying, of every tree you may eat freely, but of the tree of knowledge of good and evil, thou shall not eat of it, for in the day that thou eatest of it thou shall surely die.

You see it was Adam God spoke to first; it was Adam who was God's vice regent on earth, and I believe that God revealed this to Adam for thousands of years, and you can see that Eve was not even created yet.

Genesis 2:18

And the LORD God said, It is not good that the man should be alone; I will make him an help meet for him.

So because Adam did not properly inform Eve, she fell.

Wait a minute—what are you talking about? You have to prove that!

You see almighty God has a divine name, Yahweh, and when the serpent deceived Eve he said, "Has God indeed said...?" You will note that the serpent did not use the divine name Yahweh. Eve, not being girded properly, repeated what Satan said and not what the Lord God said. This is why in Matthew 6:9 when Jesus taught the disciples to pray He said,

"Hallowed be thy name." Eve did not hallow God's name as Lord God (Yahweh Adonai), she said God. This is how she fell into temptation. If she had said "Lord God" then Satan would not have been allowed to proceed with his allure because "Lord" means authority over all, and he would not have the ability to appeal to her reasoning.

You see, by Eve not properly hallowing God as the LORD GOD, it allowed Satan to argue that God had an ulterior motive—which was Satan's device to appeal to Eve's sense of fair play (you will be like God). God's fullness of knowledge was **ONE** of the only superiorities that set Him apart from the woman. For example in I John 3 verse 2, (Beloved, now are we the sons of God, and it doth not yet appear what we shall be: but we know that, when he shall appear, we shall be like him; for we shall see him as he is.)

John is speaking to the church about our future existence that we will be **like** GOD. Paradise lost will be paradise gain. Eve, was like GOD and the only thing that separated Adam and Eve from GOD was the fullness of knowledge. Satan, being the skilled liar that he is, combined **ALL** of God's superiority over the woman into one audacious appeal to her pride and overtook her.

Question: Where was Adam in all this? Did he see the serpent coming and decide to go fishing (things that make you go *hmmmm*)? Was he somewhere in the area waiting on Eve's

28

results? Of course he was, and Scripture aptly codifies it.

Genesis 3:6

And when the woman saw that the tree was good for food, and that it was pleasant to the eyes, and a tree desired to make one wise, she took of the fruit thereof, and did eat, and gave also unto her HUSBAND WITH HER, AND HE DID EAT.

Amos 3:3

How can two walk together unless they agree?

You see Eve took two steps:

1) She ate
2) Then she gave it to her husband with her

Notice Eve didn't die or feel convicted right away; it was when Adam ate that the world was turned upside down. What is telling is that Adam sinned with his eyes wide open; he never even asked a question, which clearly suggests that Adam didn't protect Eve for a reason. He wanted Eve to be a scapegoat, but God wanted Adam to teach Eve and grow together with her, not hinder her from studying and growing in faith. That is what Paul meant when he alluded to the garden.

Finally, why was Paul mainly talking to Timothy about women being in subjection? After all, Timothy learned the gospel from his mother and grandmother. Had Paul's intention been sexist would Timothy have received Paul's letter on fertile soil? Would he not have intractable difficulties with Paul's saying anything about female subjection after he learned the pure Word from women? The answer is a resounding **NO**. The only way Timothy would have received Paul is if Paul had an ulterior motive. What was Paul's ulterior motive?

Acts 19:20-34

²⁰So mightily grew the word of God and prevailed.

²¹After these things were ended, Paul purposed in the spirit, when he had passed through Macedonia and Achaia, to go to Jerusalem, saying, After I have been there, I must also see Rome.

²²So he sent into Macedonia two of them that ministered unto him, Timotheus and Erastus; but he himself stayed in Asia for a season.

²³And the same time there arose no small stir about that way.

²⁴For a certain man named Demetrius, a silversmith, which made silver shrines for Diana, brought no small gain unto the craftsmen;

²⁵Whom he called together with the workmen of like occupation, and said, Sirs, ye know that by this craft we have our wealth.

²⁶Moreover ye see and hear, that not alone at Ephesus, but almost throughout all Asia, this Paul hath persuaded and turned away much people, saying that they be no gods, which are made with hands:

²⁷So that not only this our craft is in danger to be set at nought; but also that the temple of the great goddess Diana should be despised, and her magnificence should be destroyed, whom all Asia and the world worship.

*28And when they heard these sayings, they were
full of wrath, and cried out, saying, Great is Diana
of the Ephesians.*

*29And the whole city was filled with confusion:
and having caught Gaius and Aristarchus, men
of Macedonia, Paul's companions in travel, they
rushed with one accord into the theatre.*

*30And when Paul would have entered in unto
the people, the disciples suffered him not.*

*31And certain of the chief of Asia, which were
his friends, sent unto him, desiring him that he
would not adventure himself into the theatre.*

*32Some therefore cried one thing, and some
another: for the assembly was confused: and the
more part knew not wherefore they were come
together.*

*33And they drew Alexander out of the multi-
tude, the Jews putting him forward. And Alexander
beckoned with the hand, and would have made his
defence unto the people.*

*34But when they knew that he was a Jew, all
with one voice about the space of two hours cried
out, Great is Diana of the Ephesians.*

Ephesus, where Timothy ministered, was the home of
an international cult dedicated to the pagan goddess Artemis
Diana. Worship of Diana was conducted under the authority
of an entirely female priesthood that exercised authoritarian
dominion over male worshippers.

So Paul's words actually refuted matriarchal authoritarian practices that the new converts brought into the church
once they were translated from darkness into the glorious
light. Many women brought their old strongholds of female
domination into the church, and when Timothy wrote Paul
about church conduct, Paul simply reciprocated by writing

an epistle God told him to write. This letter regarding women's conduct in the churches placed special emphasis on Ephesus, where Timothy was a minister and the head-quarters for Diana worship was seated.

Thus when Paul emphasized that women should not presume undue authority over men, nor men over women, he meant that men and women should be granted equal opportunity to learn and grow in submission to one another and to God.

So let it be clearly understood that God never said a woman couldn't preach or pastor a church. God was simply speaking to Paul with respect to women in the church who were not yet regenerated, who were acting out proclivities from the cult of Diana worship (speaking out of turn, usurping authority, scoffing, and the like).

Chapter 5

JUDGING THE OUTCRY
(Hypocrisy in the Pulpit)

John 8:1-11

¹Jesus went unto the mount of Olives.

²And early in the morning he came again into the temple, and all the people came unto him; and he sat down, and taught them.

³And the scribes and Pharisees brought unto him a woman taken in adultery; and when they had set her in the midst,

⁴They say unto him, Master, this woman was taken in adultery, in the very act.

⁵Now Moses in the law commanded us, that such should be stoned: but what sayest thou?

⁶This they said, tempting him, that they might have to accuse him. But Jesus stooped down, and with his finger wrote on the ground, as though he heard them not.

⁷So when they continued asking him, he lifted up himself, and said unto them, He that is without sin among you, let him first cast a stone at her.

8And again he stooped down, and wrote on the ground.

9And they which heard it, being convicted by their own conscience, went out one by one, beginning at the eldest, even unto the last: and Jesus was left alone, and the woman standing in the midst.

10When Jesus had lifted up himself, and saw none but the woman, he said unto her, Woman, where are those thine accusers? hath no man condemned thee?

11She said, No man, Lord. And Jesus said unto her, Neither do I condemn thee: go, and sin no more.

It is utterly amazing how the Pharisees had a insatiable zeal *for* the law (finger pointing) but no zeal to *perform* the law (living it).

Can you just picture the outcry in Israel two thousand years ago in this scene: when about five thousand people running to Jesus with three things in their hands—the **LAW**, **STONES**, and the **WOMAN**? Wow, did they have a zeal for God's Word. **NOT!** They forgot something—the man. According to the law that they screamed so vehemently about, "It takes two to tango."

Deuteronomy 22:23-24

23If a damsel that is a virgin be betrothed unto an husband, and a man find her in the city, and lie with her;

24Then ye shall bring them both out unto the gate of that city, and ye shall stone them with stones that they die; the damsel, because she cried not, being in the city; and the man, because he hath humbled his neighbour's wife: so thou shalt put away evil from among you.

Why didn't the crowd cry out against the co-conspirator, the man? It's simple: because the cry didn't come from the heart it came from their sexist attitudes. What was the real intent of the outcry?

1) to trap Jesus off
2) to condemn the woman

Wasn't the man equally guilty? Actually, I am wrong according to **Genesis 3:16**

[16]Unto the woman he said, I will greatly multiply thy sorrow and thy conception; in sorrow thou shalt bring forth children; and thy desire shall be to thy husband, and he shall rule over thee.

Because if the man had **ruled** properly the act would not have taken place (can somebody say *garden?*).

I have interviewed several men in the clergy and what is striking is that if I interview fifty men who are opponents of women preaching, 90 percent have an ulterior motive and the other 10 percent seriously do not understand the Scripture where God speaks through Paul on this subject. As a defense they use such verses as **Genesis 3:16**

In response to that, they didn't discern the Word spiritually: **Revelation 3:22**

He that hath an ear, let him hear what the Spirit saith unto the churches.

[Handwritten margin note, left side: Maybe You should try Translating instead of making up your own words]

Most pastors that I interviewed were convinced that what the Word said, it meant, but if that were so then I would have to retry God for being a sexist.

Let's examine it spiritually.

The word *desire* can mean to usurp or control, so we can paraphrase the last two lines like this: "You will now have a tendency to dominate your husband and he will have a tendency to act as a tyrant over you." This is where the battle of the sexes started. Each strives for control and neither lives for the best interest of the other.

The antidote is in the restoration of mutual respect and dignity through Jesus Christ.

Ephesians 5:21

Submitting yourselves to one another in the fear of God.

If you ever discuss the issue of women preaching with clergy who are against women preaching, always observe that they will use...

Ephesians 5:22-23 *[handwritten: 21 and be subject to one another in fear of Christ.]*

[22]Wives, submit yourselves unto your own husbands, as unto the Lord.

[23]For the husband is the head of the wife, even as Christ is the head of the church: and he is the saviour of the body.

...to buttress their theological judo, but what is conspicuous by its absence is verse 21.

Why not advance verse 21, because if you read verse 21 you will come to the knowledge of the truth and expose the

[Handwritten at bottom: 21. and be subject to one another in the fear of Christ.]

36

sexist mentality they received from human wisdom. Another popular verse is I read it, where is the sexist mentality???

1 Timothy 3:1-12

¹This is a true saying, if a man desire the office of a <u>bishop,</u> he desireth a good work.

²A <u>bishop</u> then must be blameless, the husband of one wife, vigilant, sober, of good behaviour, given to hospitality, apt to teach;

³Not given to wine, no striker, not greedy of filthy lucre; but patient, not a brawler, not covetous;

⁴One that ruleth well his own house, having his children in subjection with all gravity;

⁵(For if a man know not how to rule his own house, how shall he take care of the church of God?)

⁶Not a novice, lest being lifted up with pride he fall into the condemnation of the devil.

⁷Moreover he must have a good report of them which are without; lest he fall into reproach and the snare of the devil.

⁸Likewise must the <u>deacons</u> be grave, not doubletongued, not given to much wine, not greedy of filthy lucre;

⁹Holding the mystery of the faith in a pure conscience.

¹⁰And let these also first be proved; then let them use the office of a <u>deacon,</u> being found blameless.

¹¹Even so must <u>their wives</u> be grave, not slanderers, sober, faithful in all things.

¹²Let the <u>deacons be the husbands of one wife,</u> ruling their children and their own houses well.

In order to properly understand the text here you must first understand the meaning of two words.

Bishop =   A Greek word that means one who oversees the congregation.

Deacon =   Servant

Most opponents of women preaching use the word *man* or *men* to solidify their stance in this text, but if you vehemently hold *man* in that text to mean exclusively *men*, then to be honest and consistent you must be likeminded in this text.

1 Timothy 2:3-4

For this is good and acceptable in the sight of God our Saviour. Who will have all <u>men</u> to be saved, and come to the knowledge of the truth.

If you interpret **men** as all males then God is the supreme sexist and must be indicted again and brought to justice.

Additionally, if you advance this scripture for your Biblical Basis and you hold fast to the tenets therein, you would have to conclude that Paul or God was a hypocrite, because the scripture clearly says that one of the pre-requisites of a Bishop was that "he must be married to one wife, Paul was single and the Pastor of all the churches.

Why don't you tell us where in Scripture it is that Paul is the Pastor of all the churches.

Chapter 6

THE REAL DEAL ON ADAM

Let's look at the man who says a woman shouldn't preach.

Genesis 3:9-11

> *⁹And the LORD God called unto Adam, and said unto him, Where art thou?*
>
> *¹⁰And he said, I heard thy voice in the garden, and I was afraid, because I was naked; and I hid myself.*
>
> *¹¹And he said, Who told thee that thou wast naked? Hast thou eaten of the tree, whereof I commanded thee that thou shouldest not eat?*

Watch This

> *And the man said, The woman whom thou gavest to be with me, she gave me of the tree, and I did eat* (**v. 12**).

WOW!

A guilty man's first line of defense is blame. Adam had the temerity to do three things: 1) he hid from God, 2) when questioned about his transgression he blamed the woman, and 3) he blamed God.

What is so telling in **Genesis 3:6**? It states that Eve ate from the tree and **gave to her husband** *with* **her**.

Was Adam in close proximity? Yes.

To make matters worse, when confronted by God Eve came clean. God says He prefers truth in the inward parts. Listen to the discourse between Eve and God.

Genesis 3:13

And the Lord God said unto the woman, What is this that thou hast done? And the woman said, The serpent beguiled me, and I did eat.

Eve gave God a simple statement of fact.
Let's examine Adam's actions.

1) He was there
2) He knew clearly what was happening
3) He didn't stop Eve or give her the Word of God
4) He ATE
5) He ate without temptation, eyes wide open

Romans 5:12-21

[12]Wherefore, as by one man sin entered into the world, and death by sin; and so death passed upon all men, for that all have sinned:
[13](For until the law sin was in the world: but sin is not imputed when there is no law.

[Handwritten margin note: This still is not giving us any indication biblically that women can preach and teach. Still Empty]

40

[14]Nevertheless death reigned from Adam to Moses, even over them that had not sinned after the similitude of Adam's transgression, who is the figure of him that was to come.

[15]But not as the offence, so also is the free gift. For if through the offence of one many be dead, much more the grace of God, and the gift by grace, which is by one man, Jesus Christ, hath abounded unto many.

[16]And not as it was by one that sinned, so is the gift: for the judgment was by one to condemnation, but the free gift is of many offences unto justification.

[17]For if by one man's offence death reigned by one; much more they which receive abundance of grace and of the gift of righteousness shall reign in life by one, Jesus Christ.)

[18]Therefore as by the offence of one judgment came upon all men to condemnation; even so by the righteousness of one the free gift came upon all men unto justification of life.

[19]For as by one man's disobedience many were made sinners, so by the obedience of one shall many be made righteous.

[20]Moreover the law entered, that the offence might abound. But where sin abounded, grace did much more abound:

[21]That as sin hath reigned unto death, even so might grace reign through righteousness unto eternal life by Jesus Christ our Lord.

So when opponents of women preaching advance their theory that if it wasn't for Eve, Adam wouldn't have fallen, actually they are taking the biblical text out of context

Does anyone really advance this Theory??

to develop a pretext to advance their theological sexist perversion.

To say a woman was primarily at fault and is precluded from preaching at best involves a hasty generalization; at worst it is a way of poisoning the well.

Those who presuppose that women preaching is contrary to the Word should carefully consider defensible biblical arguments rather than swallow fallacious dogmatic assertions whole.

What are these defensible biblical arguments???

Chapter 7

GOD'S JUDGMENT ON WOMEN PREACHERS

At the very root of any man who says a woman cannot preach lies a seed of sexism which does not come from God, but from Satan. This is not an opinion, it is a bald fact, and I will prove it by Scripture and current events.

Whenever God speaks a command in the Bible, no matter how ambiguous it seems to you when you violate the command, God always responds with some type of calamity to show you your error and uphold His Word.

Genesis 12:3

And I will bless them that bless thee and curse them that curse thee, and in thee all the families in the earth will be blessed.

This is a prophecy regarding the *physical descendants* of Abraham, a word spoken four thousand years ago and manifested four thousand years later.

After the Gulf War ended in 1991, President Bush began the initiative to start a peace plan that would divide the land of Israel in strict defiance of God's Word in **Zechariah 2:8**

For he that touches you touches the apple of my eye.

On October 30, a powerful storm developed off Nova Scotia. The storm was never classified as a hurricane because its winds reached only 73 mph. To be classified as a hurricane, the sustained winds have to be 74 mph. This storm was extremely rare because it traveled for one thousand miles in an eastward to westward direction. The weather pattern for United States is westward to eastward. The storm was called extra-tropical because it did not originate in the tropics, as most hurricanes do.

On October 31, this ferocious storm smashed into New England. This monster of a storm was later labeled "The Perfect Storm," and a book and movie were written about it.

The storm heavily damaged President Bush's home in Kennebunkport, Maine. Eyewitnesses said that waves as high as 30 feet smashed into the president's seaport home. The president had to cancel speaking engagements to inspect the damages on his home.

Was the perfect storm a coincidence? The answer is a resounding *no*. President Bush, probably with good intentions, violated God's law and God spoke back with calamity at his doorstep.

There are two books out by John McTernan called *Israel: The Blessing or the Curse* (with Bill Koenig) and *God's Final Warning to America* that give clear examples that when a nation or people collectively disregard the Word of God, they reap harsh repercussions.

Now if women were not supposed to take a position as pastor or bishop, a logical corollary would suggest that God would be consistent with His Word by executing justice on churches shepherded by women. If you check the Internet and other databases with information on corruption or scandal in the church, however, the evidence points overwhelmingly to men.

Case in Point: 1 Timothy 4:1, 3

Now the Spirit speaketh expressly that in latter times some shall depart from the faith, giving heed to seducing spirits, and doctrines of devils, forbidding to marry...

Now God spoke this revelation to the apostle Paul 1900 years ago, and today we see its manifestation in the Catholic Church where scores of priests are caught not just in adultery and homosexuality, but also pedophilia. This was not just two or three men over a period of two decades but scores of priests in a short period of time—all because these holy men departed from God's doctrine. The end result was that God exposed their nakedness.

So the question that begs to be asked is, If women preaching is wrong, when is God going to visit this alleged apostate crime? *The Division shows its wrong*

The answer is that He has responded through the consortium of women-led churches popping up everywhere, with souls being converted. God did not curse their work. He blessed it. What a man soweth he shall reap. He who wins souls is wise. You can go from Spain to Maine debating women preaching. God's response: He responds favorably, not with fire and brimstone.

Converted to what?

In not the Lords church

You will know a tree by the fruit it bears.
This is one fig tree that JESUS did not curse.

So clearly Catholic priests refusing to marry (in direct violation of the Word of God) and being exposed through debased sexual immorality is a **blow** to the opponents of women preaching, but the fact that God didn't visit the office of women preaching with fire and brimstone is a **BULLET TO THE HEAD.**

Chapter 8

UNRINGING THE BELL

Justification

In the aforementioned chapters, the Holy Spirit reveals what Paul is saying when he states that a woman should keep silent, and why he is saying a woman should keep silent. But to those who hold fast to the doctrine that a woman shouldn't preach, it may take a bit more reasoning to unring the bell. After all, women preachers have not given a reason for their hope according to **1 Peter 3:15**

> *But sanctify the Lord God in your hearts and always be ready to give a defense for everyone who asks you a reason for the hope that is in you, with meekness and fear, having a good <u>conscience</u>, that when they defame you as evildoers, those who revile your good conduct in Christ may be ashamed.*

Most women preachers are not under spiritual conviction by their calling. For those who are called, this may be the central cause for (anti-women preachers) defaming women as evildoers, while reviling their good conduct in Christ. And because women cannot produce a good reason for their justification, instead of having a good conscience they develop a bad conscience, resulting in the scoffers never feeling ashamed but justified.

Most women, if you ask them their reason for hope, will use the garden-variety apologetics.

1) Mary Magdalene was the first woman to preach the resurrection.
2) The woman at the well preached Jesus all over Samaria.
3) Deborah was a great judge of Israel.
4) Esther delivered Israel.

These arguments and a litany of others, however true, just don't unring the bell. Why? Because there is middle ground. Whenever a subject has middle ground, there is always latitude to buttress an argument, especially for those who hold fast to a tenet they *refuse* to disbelieve, no matter how much empirical evidence is produced. As the old **motif** says, "It is very difficult to reason a person out of something he didn't reason himself into."

In my spiritual opinion, out of all the female biblical characters that women preachers advance as a reason for hope for their position, only one leaves no middle ground for conjecture, and that is **Miriam.**

Numbers 12:1-12

[1]And Miriam and Aaron spake against Moses because of the Ethiopian woman whom he had married: for he had married an Ethiopian woman.
[2]And they said, Hath the LORD indeed spoken only by Moses? hath he not spoken also by us? And the LORD heard it.

[3](Now the man Moses was very meek, above all the men which were upon the face of the earth.)

[4]And the LORD spake suddenly unto Moses, and unto Aaron, and unto Miriam, Come out ye three unto the Tabernacle of the Congregation. And the three came out.

[5]And the LORD came down in the pillar of the cloud, and stood in the door of the tabernacle, and called Aaron and Miriam: and they both came forth.

[6]And he said, Hear now my words: If there be a prophet among you, I the LORD will make myself known unto him in a vision, and will speak unto him in a dream.

[7]My servant Moses is not so, who is faithful in all mine house.

[8]With him will I speak mouth to mouth, even apparently, and not in dark speeches; and the similitude of the LORD shall he behold: wherefore then were ye not afraid to speak against my servant Moses?

[9]And the anger of the LORD was kindled against them; and he departed.

[10]And the cloud departed from off the tabernacle; and, behold, Miriam became leprous, white as snow: and Aaron looked upon Miriam, and, behold, she was leprous.

[11]And Aaron said unto Moses, Alas, my lord, I beseech thee, lay not the sin upon us, wherein we have done foolishly, and wherein we have sinned.

[12]Let her not be as one dead, of whom the flesh is half consumed when he cometh out of his mother's womb.

The question that begs to be asked is, Who was Aaron speaking to in Numbers 12:2? "Has the Lord spoken indeed only through Moses, or has He spoken to us also?" Scripture clearly codifies that the silent person in "us" was Miriam.

Question: What did Miriam, Aaron, and Moses have in common?

Answer: They all received revelation from God and taught it *publicly*. Miriam was a PREACHER. *Where is the scriptures ?*

Question: Riddle me this: How can we be certain that Miriam was a preacher?

Answer: **James 3:1**
My brethren, let not many of you become teachers, knowing that we shall receive a stricter judgment.

Question: Why did God curse Miriam with leprosy? Numbers12:1-15

    1) Answer: Because she was a preacher who received strict judgment for her disobedience.

"When they were in Hazeroth, Miriam and Aaron spoke against Moses because of the Cushite woman he had married: "He married a Cushite woman!" They said, "Has Adonai spoken only through Moses? Has God not spoken through us as well?" ... God said, "When a prophet of Adonai arises among you, I make Myself known to him in a vision. ... Not so with My servant Moses... With him I speak mouth to mouth, plainly and not in riddles..."

(Then) Miriam was stricken with snow- white scales. ... And Aaron said to Moses, "O my lord, account not to us the sin that we committed in our folly." So Moses cried out to Adonai, saying, "O God, please heal her!"

Question:	Traditionally, what is the tabernacle?
Answer:	It is the place where man meets God.
Question:	Can just any man go to the tabernacle?
Answer:	No
Question:	Which persons were specifically entitled to go in the tabernacle?
Answer:	Priests
Question:	What was the position of the priest, or put another way, what was the ostensible function of a priest?
Answer:	Counsel the people, intercede on behalf of the people, receive revelation from God, and speak publicly to the people of God regarding the revelation, offer sacrifice, go near to the Holy things.
Question:	What happened to a priest or any other person who entered the tabernacle unholy?
Answer:	He died immediately.

Exodus 28:31-35

³¹And thou shalt make the robe of the ephod all of blue.

³²And there shall be an hole in the top of it, in the midst thereof: it shall have a binding of woven work round about the hole of it, as it were the hole of an habergeon, that it be not rent.

³³And beneath upon the hem of it thou shalt make pomegranates of blue, and of purple, and of scarlet, round about the hem thereof; and bells of gold between them round about:

³⁴A golden bell and a pomegranate, a golden bell and a pomegranate, upon the hem of the robe round about.

[35]And it shall be upon Aaron to minister: and his sound shall be heard when he goeth in unto the holy place before the LORD, and when he cometh out, that he die not.

Question:	Why did the priest wear bells and have a rope tied around his waist?
Answer:	He wore bells to let the congregation know that he was alive, and he wore a belt so that if he died while in the tabernacle somebody could pull his body out.
Question:	Why couldn't one of the worshippers just go and drag him out?
Answer:	Because if they were not called by God and not sanctified by God, they would die also.
Question:	Did Miriam die when she went into the tabernacle?
Answer:	**NO**
Question:	Why not?
Answer:	Because she was called of God and specifically ordained to go in the same places as Aaron, although as a prophetess she was called to receive revelation and teach it to the people.
Question:	Wait a minute. Where does Scripture say that?
Answer:	**Micah 6:4**

For I brought thee up out of the land of Egypt, and redeemed thee out of the house of servants; and I sent before thee Moses, Aaron and MIRIAM (emphasis added).

Exactly what was Miriam's office? To follow Moses and Aaron around shouting "alleluia" or to sing a few songs? Far from that—she spoke publicly (preached) what God said to her to the first church, the Israelites, in the same manner that He speaks to the second church through women today such as:

really? Do any of these speak to the Lords church? NO they speak to Mans Church.

Roll call...

1) Dr. Marilynn Miles
2) Joyce Meyer
3) Taffy Dollar
4) Paula White
5) Juanita Bynum
6) Jackie McCullough
7) Vashti McKenzie
8) Susie Owens
9) Cheryl Brady
10) Eleanor Jones
11) Rita Twiggs
12) Medina Pullings
13) Millicent Thompson
14) Lori Screen
15) Margaret Young
16) Chairmaine Wilson
17) Rosa Drummond
18) Bonnie Bigelow
19) Caroline Hill
20) Rose Russell-Steward
21) Sheila Heath
22) Maureen Davis
23) Wilma Salford
24) Roxanne Hawkins
25) Sarah Utterbach
26) Serita Jakes
27) Corletta Vaughn
28) Betty Price

29) Sarah McLaurin
30) Francelia Derry
31) Christynne Hughes
32) Pamela McLaurin
33) Valerie Gibbs
34) Jaqueline Church
35) Annebelle Newsuan
36) Caroline Collins
37) Sandra Beecham
38) Bernice Getter
39) Caroline Bryant
40) Joyce Bell
41) Charlotte Bryant
42) Nadine White
43) Dr. Patricia Bailey

Questions and Answers

Q.   But the Bible says Miriam was only a prophetess. How does that give her permission to preach?

A.   Deuteronomy 18:15

The LORD your God will raise up for you a prophet like me from among your own brothers. You must listen to him. him is male term !!!

Q: Who was this prophet God was speaking to Moses about?
A: Jesus, the Christ.
Q: What was Jesus' *function* as a prophet?
A: **Luke 4:16-21**

[16]And he came to Nazareth, where he had been brought up: and, as his custom was, he went into

54

> *the synagogue on the Sabbath day, and stood up for to read.*
>
> *[17]And there was delivered unto him the book of the prophet Esaias. And when he had opened the book, he found the place where it was written,*
>
> *[18]The Spirit of the Lord is upon me, because he hath anointed me to preach the gospel to the poor; he hath sent me to heal the brokenhearted, to preach deliverance to the captives, and recovering of sight to the blind, to set at liberty them that are bruised,*
>
> *[19]To preach the acceptable year of the Lord.*
>
> *[20]And he closed the book, and he gave it again to the minister, and sat down. And the eyes of all them that were in the synagogue were fastened on him.*
>
> *[21]And he began to say unto them, This day is this scripture fulfilled in your ears.*

His function was to preach the gospel to the poor, heal the brokenhearted, preach deliverance to the captives, recover sight for the blind, set at liberty those who were bruised.

Q: What is the difference between a waiter and a waitress?

A: They are two people who serve food who have different **genders.**

Q: What is the difference between a prophet and a prophetess?

A: Both preach the gospel to the poor, heal the broken-hearted, preach deliverance to the captives, recover sight for the blind, and heal the bruised, but they have different **genders.**

So as the Bible illustrates, the office never changes, only the **gender** does.

You still have not shown one single example of Any Woman actually being 55 a preacher in OT or the NT. Bozo

Moreover, not only was Jesus an apostle but also Miriam. Wait a minute, minister, you are going too far.

Q: What does apostle mean?
A: One sent with a special message.
Q: Was Miriam sent by Almighty God?
A: Yes, see **Micah 6:4**

*And I sent before thee these three Moses, Aaron and **MIRIAM.***

It doesn't stretch credulity to the breaking point to surmise that Miriam had an apostolic calling, especially when God said so in **Micah 6:4**.

Clearly the word *sent* means a person with a special message or commission from God.

1 Corinthians 12:28

And in the church God has appointed first Apostles, second Prophets, third Teachers, then workers of Mracles, also those having gifts of Healing, those able to help others, those with gifts of Administration, and those speaking in different kinds of Tongues.

So in conclusion, when you read Scripture or rather interpret Scripture in light of Scripture, you will conclude that Miriam set an infallible precedent for justifying women preaching.

Chapter 9

AND THE SCRIPTURE CANNOT BE BROKEN

John 10:31-39

³¹Then the Jews took up stones again to stone him.

³²Jesus answered them, Many good works have I shewed you from my Father; for which of those works do ye stone me?

³³The Jews answered him, saying, For a good work we stone thee not; but for blasphemy; and because that thou, being a man, makest thyself God.

³⁴Jesus answered them, Is it not written in your law, I said, Ye are gods?

³⁵If he called them gods, unto whom the word of God came, and the scripture cannot be broken;

³⁶Say ye of him, whom the Father hath sanctified, and sent into the world, Thou blasphemest; because I said, I am the Son of God?

³⁷If I do not the works of my Father, believe me not.

³⁸But if I do, though ye believe not me, believe the works: that ye may know, and believe, that the Father is in me, and I in him.

³⁹Therefore they sought again to take him: but he escaped out of their hand,

This was not the first time that the Jewish leaders took up stones against Jesus. The Jewish antagonizers revealed the reason for their opposition to Jesus. Jews are fiercely monotheistic (belief in one God) and Jesus was not only claiming unique unity with the Father, He also declared that He was God. The Jewish leaders considered that blasphemy.

In the Old Testament, judges were called gods. The reason they were called gods was because they exercised god like judicial sovereignty.

Psalm 82:6

⁶I have said, Ye are gods; and all of you are children of the most High.

Psalm 82:6 the verse quoted here, refers to Judges who violate the Law. Jesus argument was that if the Divine name had been applied by God to mere men, there could be neither blasphemy nor folly in its application to the Incarnate Son of God Himself.

So when Jesus says to the Jews "And the scripture cannot be broken" This is a strong statement of the inerrancy of the Holy Scriptures notice how Jesus made the veracity if His argument rest on the absolute trustworthiness of Scripture.

If the Bible is truly the infallible inerrant Word of GOD, and Scripture cannot be broken then Jesus Christ Himself said clearly that a Holy woman can preach, and who would have the temerity to argue with Jesus the Christ.

Revelation 2:18-23

[18]And unto the angel of the church in Thyatira write; These things saith the Son of God, who hath his eyes like unto a flame of fire, and his feet are like fine brass;

[19]I know thy works, and charity, and service, and faith, and thy patience, and thy works; and the last to be more than the first.

[20]Notwithstanding I have a few things against thee, because thou sufferest that woman Jezebel, which calleth herself a prophetess, to teach and to seduce my servants to commit fornication, and to eat things sacrificed unto idols.

[21]And I gave her space to repent of her fornication; and she repented not.

[22]Behold, I will cast her into a bed, and them that commit adultery with her into great tribulation, except they repent of their deeds.

[23]And I will kill her children with death; and all the churches shall know that I am he which searcheth the reins and hearts: and I will give unto every one of you according to your works.

The question at bar is and there is no middle ground was the teacher at the church of Thyatira a woman.

Most opponents of women preaching catapult their arguments with respects to women preaching based solely on this scripture. Simultaneously when women pastors read this scripture, they shy away. Amazingly both are in error. Let's examine the test.

Q.   Exactly who was teaching in the church?
A.   A woman
Q.   Was it Jezebel?

A.   No, it was a nickname of a woman with the spirit of Jezebel.

Q.   Why was Jezebel allowed to teach?

A.   Jesus said (and scripture cannot be broken) because she called her self a prophetess

Q.   Is it true according to Jesus, in order to teach you had to qualify as a prophetess?

A.   According to Jesus Yes or He wouldn't have said it

Q.   Did Jesus rebuke the female teacher or her teaching?

A.   He rebuked her teaching.

Q.   How can we be certain?

A.   Because in verse 21 Christ gave her time to repent not of her preaching, but what she was teaching.

How does he make that conclusion??

In the nutshell, Jesus approved of a female teacher at Thyatira. Just not the apostate doctrine that she taught. The question at bar is, if the woman preacher at Thyatira wasn't teaching an apostate doctrine would have Jesus rebuked her? The answer is clear **NO**. So if Jesus is the Head of the church and clearly He affirmed this woman's office what human on Earth has the temerity to come against the Holy One of Israel.

Chapter 10

HOW LONG ARE WE GOING TO FALTER BETWEEN TWO OPINIONS

1ˢᵀ Kings 18:21

²¹And Elijah came unto all the people, and said, How long halt ye between two opinions? if the LORD be God, follow him: but if Baal, then follow him. And the people answered him not a word.

The Great prophet Elijah was entangled with a huge spiritual contest at Mt. Carmel.

It was a contest between the Lord and a false god named Baal. The competition involved who was the God of the storm. As you observed in vs. 38,39 Elijah proved who was the True and Living God but although Elijah proved empirically that the LORD was the true God of heaven and the people testified to it that the Lord was God. Nevertheless, through the centuries although proven to be false, Baal was worshipped as God.

These words spoken over 2,800 years ago "How long are we going to falter between two opinions are still resonating in the world through world Religion (Buddhism, Judaism, Islam, Hinduism, etc.) and unfortunately, it is resonating in the church.

The Battle

Can a woman preach?
Vs.
Let a woman preach

As in any sport or competition there are rules, regulations, and a referee, underscored below are the rules and regulations **THE HOLY SPIRIT IS THE REFEREE.**

All scripture is to be interpreted in its historical context.

All scripture is to be interpreted in light of the verses surrounding it.

All scripture is to be interpreted in light of the overall message of scripture. Since God's word cannot contradict itself, any interpretation that violates other scripture on the same subject cannot be correct.

Round 1
Let a woman preach.

If Paul says in **1ˢᵗ Timothy 2:12, 1st Corinthians 14:35** and the bevy of other scriptures were interpreted in its most literal sense and this is what the Spirit literally means then any male Pastor who allows a woman to sing, verbally praise, teach Sunday school is in serious sin.

1ˢᵗ Timothy 2:12

¹²But I suffer not a woman to teach, nor to usurp authority over the man, but to be in silence

1ˢᵗ Corinthians 14:35

³⁵And if they will learn anything, let them ask their husbands at home: for it is a shame for women to speak in the church.

Moreover to ask a Pastor to sin is opening the door for sin (sin lies at the door)

So why don't we ask the Pastor to adjoin us to other married couples surreptiously which is adultery and to teach a doctrine supporting fornication and to create a system that will allow us to cheat on our taxes. Hey sin is sin right.

Additionally, let us go straight to Pastors who teach with women preachers, Creflo Dollar, T.D. Jakes, Eddie Long, John Hagee and the like and declare to them like John the Baptist declared to Herod that they are in sin. How could we let these counterfeits (if you say that women should not preach) loom on the horizon unabated? Easy. Because we have no sound Biblical foundation to support our antithetical thinking.

You see to ask the question can women preach is to confuse categories. In the Great Timely words of Anne Graham Lotz, Billy Graham's daughter when asked can a woman preach she responded, "Well, you know, I feel like I am not accountable to them. I am accountable to God and His call on my life, and I believe each of us needs to study the scriptures ourselves to determine what we believe."

Well that brings me to this scripture in **Romans 16:7**

[7]Salute Andronicus and Junia, my kinsmen, and my fellow-prisoners, who are of note among the apostles, who also were in Christ before me.

Who was Junias if you read by rules Junias is feminine which suggest that she is the wife of Andronicus not only was she an Apostle but one of Great note. What's your opinion? In **Acts 18:24-26** we read a lady by the name of Priscilla, who along with her husband Aquila, expounded the way of God more perfectly to a brilliant Jewish man named Apollos, who would later become a preacher of the Gospel, until Priscilla and Aquila taught him. He only knew the baptism of John. As scripture says so clearly in **Acts 18:26** they took him unto them (Priscilla & Aquila) and expounded unto him the way of God more perfectly.

Acts 18:24-26

[24]And a certain Jew named Apollos, born at Alexandria, an eloquent man, and mighty in the scriptures, came to Ephesus.
[25]This man was instructed in the way of the Lord; and being fervent in the spirit, he spake and taught diligently the things of the Lord, knowing only the baptism of John.
[26]And he began to speak boldly in the synagogue: whom when Aquila and Priscilla had heard, they took him unto them, and expounded unto him the way of God more perfectly.

If **1st Timothy 2:12** was literally intended to totally forbid women from teaching men then Apollos was **sinning** by accepting spiritual guidance from Priscilla. What is your opinion?

Last but not least Phillip's daughters **Acts 21:9** says that Phillip the evangelist had four daughters who were prophets. The term used here is taken from the same root word used in **Acts 15:32** to describe two male prophets, Judas and Silas.

Acts 21:9

⁹And the same man had four daughters, virgins, which did prophesy.

Acts 15:32

³²And Judas and Silas, being prophets also themselves, exhorted the brethren with many words, and confirmed them.

We know nothing about the daughters but we can logically deduce that their influence was significant enough to be mentioned in Biblical Record. Obviously they were engaged into public speaking and their message carried the same authority as Agabus a male prophet mentioned in **Acts 21:10** Phillip's daughters were in essence, women preachers who experienced a high level of respect for their spiritual insights and high level of giftedness. What is your opinion?

Acts 21:10

¹⁰And as we tarried there many days, there came down from Judaea a certain prophet, named Agabus

So in conclusion, the question at bar is can a woman preach? What is your opinion?

If **Joel 2:28** read like this

In the last days, I will pour out my Spirit, and your sons will prophesy while your daughters serve quietly in the background and pray for men.

I would agree with the opponents of women preachers, but since it reads like this

Joel 2:28

[28]And it shall come to pass afterward, that I will pour out my spirit upon all flesh; and your sons and your daughters shall prophesy, your old men shall dream dreams, your young men shall see visions:

I am of the clear opinion that God ordained women to preach no more faltering.

James 1:8

A double-minded man is unstable in all his ways.

Chapter 11

THE LEVELING OF THE PLAYING FIELD

(Why women were not called to be Priest in the Old Testament)

When I first started to write this manuscript I hit a bump in the road that caused me to second guess my theology. This bump caused me to go in deep water with respects to my studying the subject of women preaching. The question was asked by a group of erudite male preachers while at a picnic in Lehigh County and they asked the profound question

Why weren't there any women in the Old Testament Priesthood? Brilliant questions deserves equally brilliant responses, but I was stuck, but when I went to the playing field as always God leveled it out.

Why couldn't a woman hold the office of a Priestess?

Essential Idea of Priesthood

Moses furnishes us with the key to the Old Testament priesthood in **Numbers 16:5** which consist of 3 elements

Numbers 16:5;

Numbers 16:5

⁵And He spoke unto Korah and unto all his company, saying, Even tomorrow the Lord will show who are His and who is holy; and will cause him to come near to Him; even him who He hath chosen will he cause to come near unto Him.

1) Being chosen and set apart for Jehovah as His own
2) Being Holy
3) Being allowed to come near to Holy things

The first expresses the fundamental condition
The second expresses the qualification
The third expresses the function of the priesthood
Let us focus on the 3rd pre-requisite coming near to Holy things.

1st Samuel 21:1-6

¹Then came David to Nob to Ahimelech the priest: and Ahimelech was afraid at the meeting of David, and said unto him, Why art thou alone, and no man with thee?
²And David said unto Ahimelech the priest, The king hath commanded me a business, and hath said unto me, Let no man know any thing of the business whereabout I send thee, and what I have commanded thee: and I have appointed my servants to such and such a place.
³Now therefore what is under thine hand? give me five loaves of bread in mine hand, or what there is present.

⁴And the priest answered David, and said, There is no common bread under mine hand, but there is hallowed bread; if the young men have kept themselves at least from women.

⁵And David answered the priest, and said unto him, Of a truth women have been kept from us about these three days, since I came out, and the vessels of the young men are holy, and the bread is in a manner common, yea, though it were sanctified this day in the vessel.

⁶So the priest gave him hallowed bread: for there was no bread there but the shewbread, that was taken from before the LORD, to put hot bread in the day when it was taken away.

Q.   Why did Abimelech ask David if he was kept from women?

A.   It was something impure about a woman that precluded them from entering the Temple.

Q.   Why did David respond yes but went on to say for about 3 days?

A.   Because the woman could have been ritually impure by her God given menstrual cycle.

Q.   Can you support that Biblically

A.   **Leviticus 15:19-28**

¹⁹And if a woman have an issue, and her issue in her flesh be blood, she shall be put apart seven days: and whosoever toucheth her shall be unclean until the even.

²⁰And every thing that she lieth upon in her separation shall be unclean: every thing also that she sitteth upon shall be unclean.

[21]*And whosoever toucheth her bed shall wash his clothes, and bathe himself in water, and be unclean until the even.*

[22]*And whosoever toucheth any thing that she sat upon shall wash his clothes, and bathe himself in water, and be unclean until the even.*

[23]*And if it be on her bed, or on any thing whereon she sitteth, when he toucheth it, he shall be unclean until the even.*

[24]*And if any man lie with her at all, and her flowers be upon him, he shall be unclean seven days; and all the bed whereon he lieth shall be unclean.*

[25]*And if a woman have an issue of her blood many days out of the time of her separation, or if it run beyond the time of her separation; all the days of the issue of her uncleanness shall be as the days of her separation: she shall be unclean.*

[26]*Every bed whereon she lieth all the days of her issue shall be unto her as the bed of her separation: and whatsoever she sitteth upon shall be unclean, as the uncleanness of her separation.*

[27]*And whosoever toucheth those things shall be unclean, and shall wash his clothes, and bathe himself in water, and be unclean until the even.*

[28]*But if she be cleansed of her issue, then she shall number to herself seven days, and after that she shall be clean.*

Q.   Do you have additional Biblical information to help your theory?

A.   Yes. **Mark 5:25-34**

[25]*And a certain woman, which had an issue of blood twelve years,*

²⁶*And had suffered many things of many physicians, and had spent all that she had, and was nothing bettered, but rather grew worse,*
²⁷*When she had heard of Jesus, came in the press behind, and touched his garment.*
²⁸*For she said, If I may touch but his clothes, I shall be whole.*
²⁹*And straightway the fountain of her blood was dried up; and she felt in her body that she was healed of that plague.*
³⁰*And Jesus, immediately knowing in himself that virtue had gone out of him, turned him about in the press, and said, Who touched my clothes?*
³¹*And his disciples said unto him, Thou seest the multitude thronging thee, and sayest thou, Who touched me?*
³²*And he looked round about to see her that had done this thing.*
³³*But the woman fearing and trembling, knowing what was done in her, came and fell down before him, and told him all the truth.*
³⁴*And he said unto her, Daughter, thy faith hath made thee whole; go in peace, and be whole of thy plague.*

Q. Who was this woman?

A. A Jewish woman who suffered with a menstruation cycle for 12 years and was declared unclean.

Q. Why did she come to Jesus?

A. Because like most people when we run out of options we choose God (Whoever calls on the Lord will be saved)

Q. Did Jesus heal her?

A. Yes

Q. Why did Jesus heal her?

A.   Because of her faith.

Q.   What was so exceptional about her faith?

A.   By the law this woman was unclean and in total violation of touching anything or anybody yet she pressed through the crowd, additionally when she touched Christ (The Holy One of Israel) by law she really made a huge mistake but the scripture says that Christ looked around to see who had done this thing, but the woman fearing and trembling knowing what had happened to her, came and fell down before Him and told Him the whole truth.

Q.   What was the whole truth?

A.   This Jewish woman stooped down and told Jesus that she believed that He was the **NEW COVENANT.**

Q.   Please explain

A.   In the book of **Leviticus chapter 15** God gave Moses the law that a woman would be ritually impure after 7 days if she continued to bleed.

Q.   Where did Moses receive the law?

A.   Mount Horeb in Egypt.

Q.   Was this woman a Jew?

A.   Yes she was called Daughter that means of the flesh of Abraham.

Q.   Was she under the law?

A.   Yes

Q.   Well then how did she communicate to Jesus that He was the **NEW COVENANT?**

A.   **Jeremiah 31:31-34**

[31]Behold, the days come, saith the LORD, that I will make a new covenant with the house of Israel, and with the house of Judah:
[32]Not according to the covenant that I made with their fathers in the day that I took them by the hand

> *to bring them out of the land of Egypt; which my*
> *covenant they brake, although I was an husband*
> *unto them, saith the LORD:*
> *[33]But this shall be the covenant that I will make*
> *with the house of Israel; After those days, saith the*
> *LORD, I will put my law in their inward parts, and*
> *write it in their hearts; and will be their God, and*
> *they shall be my people.*
> *[34]And they shall teach no more every man his*
> *neighbour, and every man his brother, saying,*
> *Know the LORD: for they shall all know me, from*
> *the least of them unto the greatest of them, saith the*
> *LORD: for I will forgive their iniquity, and I will*
> *remember their sin no more.*

You see according to **Leviticus 15** a woman was unclean when she bled and couldn't come near holy things. In **Jeremiah 31** God promised a **NEW CONVENANT.** So when the woman touched him unclean she demonstrated to Him that she believed that He was the **NEW COVENANT** and HE confirmed that HE was the NEW COVENANT by blessing the woman and healing the issue of blood.

Matthew 26:26-28

> *[26]And as they were eating, Jesus took bread, and*
> *blessed it, and brake it, and gave it to the disciples,*
> *and said, Take, eat; this is my body.*
> *[27]And he took the cup, and gave thanks, and*
> *gave it to them, saying, Drink ye all of it;*
> *[28]For this is my blood of the new testament,*
> *which is shed for many for the remission of sins.*

So in conclusion by the unclean woman publicly touching a Rabbi (Jesus) this demonstrated that Jesus was the fulfillment of **Jeremiah 31:31-34.**

Moreover, God in His Divine Sovereignty not only allowed women to come near the Priesthood, but He even allowed a woman to conceive **THE HOLY ONE OF ISRAEL, CHRIST THE HIGH PRIEST.** How much closer can you come?

So the question is not why women were not Priest in the Old Testament, but how did they become Priest in the New Testament.

Since Christ is the end of the law for everyone who believes as the woman with the issue of blood so eloquently demonstrated the woman is not only free from her ritual impurity and able to come near the holy things but now she can perform her priestly duties according to Peter in **1ˢᵗ Peter 2:1-5, 9-10**

1ˢᵗ Peter 2:1-5, 9-10

Wherefore laying aside all malice, and all guile, and hypocrisies, and envies, and all evil speakings,
²As newborn babes, desire the sincere milk of the word, that ye may grow thereby:
³If so be ye have tasted that the Lord is gracious.
⁴To whom coming, as unto a living stone, disallowed indeed of men, but chosen of God, and precious,
⁵Ye also, as lively stones, are built up a spiritual house, an holy Priesthood, to offer up spiritual sacrifices, acceptable to God by Jesus Christ.
⁹But ye are a chosen generation, a royal Priesthood, an holy nation, a peculiar people; that ye should shew forth the praises of him who hath

called you out of darkness into his marvellous light;
   [10]Which in time past were not a people, but are now the people of God: which had not obtained mercy, but now have obtained mercy.

No theologian with a sober scholarship about Christian theology should have the cheek to debate this. Clearly Peter affirms a woman's priesthood to interpret any other way would be demonstratively sexist.

Wait a minute minister, just wait one minute. I see not only a contradiction in your theology but an apparent contradiction. You said in this text that the only reason that GOD did not chose women as priest in the Old Testament was because of the issue of blood..

Well you contradicted yourself because in the chapter Unringing the Bell, you said that Miriam went in the Holy of Holies and did not die. Well how could she do that if you said those women were prohibited from going inside the tabernacle? Was not Miriam a woman and did not she bleed. Can you explain that apparent contradiction?

The answer is yes and the text is not contradictory put in another way, it is complimentary. It actually harmonizes with this chapter.

Let us begin surgery on your question, which was brilliant, clearly brilliant questions deserved

Equally brilliant responses.

QUESTION:

Q. When was Moses born?
A. Around 1500 B.C.
Q. When did he start his ministry?
A. Eighty Years after his birth
Q. Did Moses have a sister?

A.   Yes, Miriam
Q.   Was she older than Moses?
A.   Yes
Q.   How much older?
A.   The Bible does not say
Q.   Can you make an educated guess?
A.   Yes between 81 and 100 years
Q.   How did you come to that conclusion?
A.   Well numbers continue the journey of Exodus, beginning with the second

Month of the second year. Numbers 10:11 11 and ending with the eleventh month of the fortieth year. Therefore, a conservative estimation would place Miriam's age between 81-100 years old.

"And it came to pass on the twentieth day of the second month, in the second year, that the cloud was taken up from the tabernacle of the testimony."

Q.   In the book of Genesis 18:1-13 God appeared to Abraham and Sarah in the form of a theophany and GOD told Sarah that she would conceive children. Why did Sarah laugh?
A.   Because she passed the age of childbearing.
Q.   What must a woman have to bear children?
A.   A period (blood)
Q.   How old was Sarah?
A.   According to scripture Gen. 17:17-21

17Then Abraham fell upon his face and laughed, and said in his heart, "Shall a child be born unto him that is a hundred years old? And shall Sarah, who is ninety years old, bear?"

18And Abraham said unto God, "O that Ishmael might live before Thee!"

19And God said, "Sarah thy wife shall bear thee a son indeed, and thou shalt call his name Isaac; and I will establish my covenant with him for an everlasting covenant, and with his seed after him.

20And as for Ishmael, I have heard thee. Behold, I have blessed him, and will make him fruitful and will multiply him exceedingly. Twelve princes shall he beget, and I will make him a great nation.

21But my covenant will I establish with Isaac, whom Sarah shall bear unto thee at this set time in the next year."

Sarah was 91 years old when she conceived Isaac.

Q.   Is it logical that like Sarah who was about the same age as Miriam, that Miriam's issue of blood was biologically cut off?

A.   Yes

Now because Miriam was the only woman that we see in scripture go into the Holies of Holies in the Old testament and she was not called until her early to mid eighties. It only serves to compliment the theory that the only thing that kept women from the priesthood was the Blood.

Miriam stopped bleeding.

Chapter 12

SUBTLE SEXISM

The following excerpt is one of a pantheon of dissertations promoting the theory that a woman does not have a place in the pulpit. I caution you to read with an open mind, but not so open that all reasoning falls out. Put another way, read this dissertation in *light of Scripture*.

According to David Cloud, he believes that

The Bible states that the man is to lead in the home and church, and the woman's role is to submit to the man's headship. He says that there is widespread rebellion against this divine plan, though, and many women are being appointed to leadership positions in churches. He ask you to Consider some facts from:

There are almost 4,000 licensed and ordained women in the Assemblies of God.

In 1984 the Southern Baptist Convention adopted a resolution saying the Bible "excludes women from pastoral leadership." Like many things adopted by this Convention, the resolution was almost meaningless. In a September 1993 meeting of the SBC Executive Committee, a measure to expel congregations for ordaining women was rejected unanimously. The Fall 1997 edition of Folio, the news-letter of Baptist Women in Ministry, reported that there are 1,225 ordained Southern Baptist women. Roughly 200 of the ordained women serve as pastors and associate pastors. In 1979 there were only 58 ordained Southern Baptist women, but the number has increased rapidly in the 1980's and 1990's, during the same period in which the "conservatives" have dominated the national convention.

The United Methodist Church has ordained women since 1956 and today has 4,743 women "clergy."

The Presbyterian Church (U.S.A.) has 2,419 female leaders. In 1979 the United Presbyterian Church, fore-runner of the Presbyterian Church U.S.A., adopted a resolu-tion REQUIRING the congregations to elect women elders. This politically correct denomination also voted to ban the ordination of any man who opposed women clergy and gave such men 10 years to change their minds or get out (EP News Service, June 21, 1980). So much for the supposed broad-minded attitude of Modernists.

The United Church of Christ has 1,803 female leaders.

The Evangelical Lutheran Church in America has 1,358 ordained women.

As of 1992, 15 of the 30 independent Anglican commu-nions around the world had approved ordination of women priests. The Episcopal Church in the United States, which approved women's ordination in 1976, has 1,070. The Episcopalians ordained the first Anglican female bishop in 1989. Though the "mother church" in England has not yet ordained women priests, the Church of England General Synod endorsed the concept of female priests in 1989 and they are moving rapidly toward finalization of the prac-tice. In 1991 Queen Elizabeth showed her approval of this by appointing a woman as one of her royal chaplains in Scotland.

The Church of Scotland approved the ordination of women in 1968 and now has 100 female ministers.

The Lutheran Church-Missouri Synod, though more conservative than other Lutheran bodies, is beginning to allow women to preach in regular worship services. A survey showed that about 1,000 LCMS clergymen maintain that the Bible is not opposed to the ordination of women (Christian News, Feb. 13, 1989).

"Leaders of Youth With a Mission (YWAM) appointed their first female national director in March to oversee a 200-member staff in Switzerland. At a conference last year, YWAM founder Loren Cunningham spoke out strongly against what he called 'cultural bias' against women. He also warned that God's blessing might be removed if YWAM did not commission female leaders" (Charisma, July 1993).

"Women now comprise at least a third of the student population at the leading interdenominational divinity schools; at Yale and Harvard, they're more than half" (Ibid.).

"U.S. women ordained to full-time ministry in 1986 increased to 20,730 from 10,470 in 1977, and represented 7.9% of all U.S. clergy, according to the recent study by the National Council of Churches. ...The survey showed that 84 of 166 denominations ordain women to full ministry... (National & International Religion Report, March 13, 1989).

These statistics do not pose a moral threat to our society. Instead it leaves room for more souls to be saved than ever.

Sadly, the church is always affected by society. Thus the rebellion of women in the world is causing similar problems in the churches, and we find women demanding leadership roles in many Christian groups.

He feels that The Bible speaks too clearly on this subject for there to be any confusion. He states that the problem is that churches too often are looking to sources other than the Bible for guidance. God loves women as much as He does men. Women are as important to the home, church, and society as men are. In Jesus Christ, women enjoy the same spiritual position and blessings before God as men do.

So we agree on this. This is the real Biblical thought on the women's role. Now read how he adds his "world view".

This does not mean, though, there is to be no difference in men and women in their appearance and roles. There is a basic truth which needs to be restated in the church and society today: Men and women are different!

Men and women were made for different roles. (world view). **Biblical view (when Moses did not obey God and circumsized his son, God threatened to kill Moses. Moses wife who did not want to see her husband die, circumsizes her son out of obedience to God and God counted it as sufficient enough to allow Moses to live.**

"And it came to pass by the way in the inn, that the LORD met him (Moses), and sought to kill him. *Then Zipporah took a sharp stone, and cut off the foreskin of her son, and cast [it] at his feet, and said, Surely a bloody husband [art] thou to me. So he let him go: then she said, A bloody husband [thou art], because of the circumcision." (Exodus 4:18-26)*

So he continues, The New Testament affirms that men are to be the leaders in the home, church, and state. Women were not created to rule these divine institutions; men were.

"Priscilla and Aquila... took him aside and explained the Way of God to him more accurately." (Acts 18:26, NRSV). My DEAR BROTHER, it was Not just Aquila, but scripture clearly states that it was Pricilla and Aquila.

Now our dear brother goes on to say,

The prophet Isaiah was condemning Israel when he said women ruled over them (Isa. 3:12). In the church, according to the Bible, no woman is qualified to be a pastor or a deacon or in any other leadership position over men. Who says? God says! He states adamantly.

At first blush, an untrained eye will read this man's oratory, and say *wow this man of God is on point,* but in all truth, this man's thesis is commensurate to the Pharisees attempting to condemn Jesus (God Incarnate).

Luke 14:1-6 (KJV)

[1]And it came to pass, as he went into the house of one of the chief Pharisees to eat bread on the sabbath day, that they watched him.

[2]And, behold, there was a certain man before him which had the dropsy.

[3]And Jesus answering spake unto the lawyers and Pharisees, saying, Is it lawful to heal on the sabbath day?

[4]And they held their peace. And he took him, and healed him, and let him go;

[5]And answered them, saying, Which of you shall have an ass or an ox fallen into a pit, and will not straightway pull him out on the sabbath day?

[6]And they could not answer him again to these things.

Exodus 20:8-10 (KJV)

Remember the Sabbath day, to keep it holy.

Six days shalt thou labour, and do all thy work: But the seventh day is the Sabbath of the LORD thy God: in it thou shalt not do any work, thou, nor thy son, nor thy daughter, thy manservant, nor thy maidservant, nor thy cattle, nor thy stranger that is within thy gates...

You see the scribes, Pharisees, and lawyers dared not speak because according to the law they had a point but according to the spirit they sinned. How did you come to that conclusion? Easy.

The scribes saw Jesus heal a man with dropsy, but instead of lauding Him for His work, they quickly attempted to condemn Jesus for the manner and means with which He did the work. They never considered the weightier matter. They gave the Sabbath more weight than a person's life. So what Jesus tested their hearts spiritually. He put the ball in their court. When the scribes pictured losing a $500 donkey they had a change of heart with respect to the law.

In the same manner, men who oppose women preaching mirror the image of the Pharisees. They do not take Scripture and read it for all it's worth. Put another way, they recite Scripture in a very grandiloquent manner, repackaging it to make you think they are zealous for God's will and then hold it over women's heads to create an atmosphere of superiority over their souls. You know it does not matter how liltingly Snow White is portrayed; it is still just a fairy tale.

Clearly if this Pastor was really zealous to hear what the Spirit says in Isaiah 3:12 he would have studied the scripture.

If he would have studied the scripture he would have went line by line, precept by precept and understand clearly what God was saying to the church, was the prophet Isaiah condemning Israel when he said women would rule over them. Is it really true that in the church no woman is qualified to Pastor or deacon in any leadership role? Did God say that?

The answers to the litany of questions is, the Pastor's theory is demonstratively false and to prove it we will do surgery on the Scripture **2 Timothy 3:16.**

[16]All scripture is given by inspiration of God, and is profitable for doctrine, for reproof, for correction, for instruction in righteousness:

Isaiah 3:12

[12]As for my people, children are their oppressors, and women rule over them. O my people, they which lead thee cause thee to err, and destroy the way of thy paths.

Let's examine the entire text of **Isaiah 3:1-12.**

[1]For, behold, the Lord, the LORD of hosts, doth take away from Jerusalem and from Judah the stay and the staff, the whole stay of bread, and the whole stay of water.
[2]The mighty man, and the man of war, the judge, and the prophet, and the prudent, and the ancient,
[3]The captain of fifty, and the honorable man, and the counselor, and the cunning artificer, and the eloquent orator.
[4]And I will give children to be their princes, and babes shall rule over them.
[5]And the people shall be oppressed, everyone by another, and every one by his neighbour: the child shall behave himself proudly against the ancient, and the base against the honorable.
[6]When a man shall take hold of his brother of the house of his father, saying, Thou hast clothing,

be thou our ruler, and let this ruin be under thy hand:

⁷In that day shall he swear, saying, I will not be a healer; for in my house is neither bread nor clothing: make me not a ruler of the people.

⁸For Jerusalem is ruined, and Judah is fallen: because their tongue and their doings are against the LORD, to provoke the eyes of his glory.

⁹The shew of their countenance doth witness against them; and they declare their sin as Sodom, they hide it not. Woe unto their soul! for they have rewarded evil unto themselves.

¹⁰Say ye to the righteous, that it shall be well with him: for they shall eat the fruit of their doings.

¹¹Woe unto the wicked! it shall be ill with him: for the reward of his hands shall be given him.

¹²As for my people, children are their oppressors, and women rule over them. O my people, they which lead thee cause thee to err, and destroy the way of thy paths.

The text clearly speaks about Judgment on Judah and Jerusalem and you would have to make the scripture stand on all four to make it mean what this beloved Pastor says it mean. Women

Pastoring is foreign to the text.

When the Scripture spoke in Isaiah 3:12 God used a hyperbole (an exaggerated term) to demonstrate his disgust on the ungodly leaders in Judah and Jerusalem.

Judah's administration was organized around warriors, mighty men, captain of fifties, elders, counselors, etc. These positions were overwhelmingly masculine. So when God condescended to speak to Isaiah he was not <u>once</u> <u>again</u> condemning women positioning in the kingdom.

Put in another way he condemned Judah and Jerusalem secular system by comparing its leadership to be reduced to an effeminate one or more over when the text read that they would be replaced by children and babes scripture denoted that their leadership would be replaced by inexperienced, incompetent leadership.

In conclusion, you would have to torture scripture to make it mean what this dear Pastor says it mean and unfortunately he did.

2 Corinthians 3:6 (KJV)

Who also hath made us able ministers of the New Testament; not of the letter, but of the spirit: for the letter killeth, but the spirit giveth life.

For years, women have been looked upon as second-class citizens, stigmatized as sex tools, cooks, and laundry maids. Thank God for Margaret Thatcher, Oprah Winfrey, Condoleezza Rice, and Mary McLaurin or I may have embraced this empirically fallacious ideology also.

Just as the secular world has embraced sexism, so has the church.

Chapter 13

THE LETTER KILLS

When a person reads Scripture by the letter he or she always runs into the problem of interpreting Scripture by the flesh. It means that you receive and espouse revelation from a fallen mind as opposed to a holy mind, which is the mind of God.

Case in Point: When men read…

Genesis 3:16

To the woman he said, "I will greatly increase your pains in childbearing; with pain you will give birth to children. Your desire will be for your husband, and he will rule over you."

Ephesians 5:22-23

Wives, submit to your husbands as to the Lord. For the husband is the head of the wife as Christ is the head of the church, his body, of which he is the Savior.

Hebrews 13:7, 17

Remember your leaders, who spoke the word of God to you. Consider the outcome of their way of life and imitate their faith.

Obey your leaders and submit to their authority. They keep watch over you as men who must give an account. Obey them so that their work will be a joy, not a burden, for that would be of no advantage to you.

Immediately we read words like *rule*, *submit*, and *the head* and we come under the odd predilection that God thinks like us. This is our thinking:

Rule = to dominate, control, dictate
Head = to lead, always be first
Submit = to have supremacy over, to yield in a conde-
        scending manner

This is the way God interprets the words:

Hebrews 13:17

What is God saying in these Scripture passages when He says obey, submit, and rule? God is simply saying that your minister (male or female) will have to be accountable for their service to you at the judgment seat of Christ.

God is saying when your Pastor rules over your soul whether it be a male Pastor or female Pastor the word rule in the kingdom system is mutually exclusive from rule in the secular world system.

Example:

If Sadaam Hussein rules Iraq as a dictatorship the citizens of Iraq have to obey his rules whether they like it or not or suffer the penalty even if it is terrorism or the ultimate which is death.

When God uses the word **Rule** it is not secular, it is spiritual.

Example: Pastor Joyce Myers (or any female Pastor) has a saint that is a delivered degenerate gambler that has a propensity to spend too much time down Atlantic City; he consults her by conviction of his conscience.

She then ministers to the troubled saint by way of **2 Peter 2:20-22.**

> *20For if after they have escaped the pollutions of the world through the knowledge of the Lord and Savior Jesus Christ, they are again entangled therein, and overcome, the latter end is worse with them than the beginning.*
>
> *21For it had been better for them not to have known the way of righteousness, than, after they have known it, to turn from the holy commandment delivered unto them.*
>
> *22But it is happened unto them according to the true proverb, the dog is turned to his own vomit again; and the sow that was washed to her wallowing in the mire.*

He receives the revelation submits to it and become a blessing to his family and community.

So the word rule in scripture actually mean responsible. What is the Pastor male or female responsible for? They are responsible for leading you to the path of **righteousness.**

Likewise, the word submits and head. The word submit in a spiritual text means to willfully render to the Spirit of God, adversely receiving a blessing.

Head or headship is a Greek terminology, which interpreted in the Greek as Kephale, which means of relation to his wife.

Let us discuss headship from a biblical perspective. Exactly what is headship? I Corinthians 11:3

3But I would have you know that the head of every man is Christ, and the head of the woman is the man, and the head of Christ is God.

When the term head is used metaphorically, the head primarily means leadership, as it is used in this passage. This is clear. I believe from 3-fold use of it that the apostle makes here. The one in controversy is the second one. "The head of the woman is her husband," but he brackets this with two examples of headship so that we might understand from them what the middle one means.

The 1st one "the head of everyman is Christ." There we see the declaration of Christ right to lead the whole human race. Christ is the leader of the race, the One to be followed.

Now let us move down to the 3rd level of headship mentioned here, "the Head of Christ is GOD." Here we see the manifestation of Leadership demonstrated in history. Jesus, the Son of GOD, equal to the Father in deity, nevertheless when he assumes humanity, He voluntarily submits Himself to the Father.

John 4:34

34Jesus said unto them, "My meat is to do the will of Him that sent Me, and to finish His work.

John 14:28

28Ye have heard how I said unto you, `I go away and come again unto you.' If ye loved Me, ye would* *rejoice because I said, `I go unto the Father,' for My Father is greater than I.

That does not challenge the equality of the members of the GOD-head, when Christ became man He voluntarily consented to take a lower position than the Father. In a sense He says, "My Father is greater than I.

These two headships help us understand the central headship. "The head of the woman is the man. Most males and I must confess I was one of them were under the odd predilection that women were our GOD ordained personal slaves and I was comfortable with my thinking but when I read scripture in light of scripture my theology was turned upside down.

In order for me to make my point with the central head-ship, "the head of every woman is a man," I am forced to jump to a few other scriptures that actually have Bible readers BOUND when it comes to what God said about the sexes., specifically women (I Cor. 11:7-9, 1 Cor. 11:4-6).

4 Every man praying or prophesying with his head covered disgraced his head. 5 But every woman praying or prophesying with her head not covered disgraced her head: for it is all one as if she were shaven. 6 For if a woman be not covered, let her be shorn. But if it be a shame to a woman to be shorn or made bald, let her cover her head. 7 The man indeed ought not to cover his head: because he is the image and glory of God. But the woman is the glory of the man. 8 For the man is not of the woman: but the woman of the man. 9 For the man was not created for the woman: but the woman for the man.

The principle of headship is something true from the very beginning of humankind. Paul labors to say that in the beginning man was made in the image and glory of God. Image is the full manifestation of something. In this case, it is God Himself.

What we must bear clearly in mind is that, when Genesis states the man was made in God's image, it was made before the two sexes were separated. Adam was first created, and it was of Adam, before Eve was separated from him, that it is said that man is the image of the Glory of God.

This means that **after** the separation woman shares the Glory and Image of God equally with the male. They are both included when scripture said that man was made in the image and the glory of God. That is why in Genesis 5 (not Genesis 1) it says that God created them in the beginning, male and female, and he named them Adam. God did not name them the Adam's he named them Adam. Therefore, the woman bears equally with the male the image and Glory of God. The male, however, is called upon to manifest certain aspects of the glory of God different from that of the woman, which brings this in mind:

1 Corinthians 11:11-12
11 But yet neither is the man without the woman, nor the woman without the man, in the Lord. 12 For as the woman is of the man, so also is the man by the woman: but all things of God.

Here is a very positive statement of fact demonstrating the full equality (as persons) of men and women. If you observe there is not a hint of inferiority involved no matter what destructive heresies that has crept into the church to reduce women to inferior status, this scripture gets it straight.

1 Cor. 11:4-6
4 Every man praying or prophesying with his head covered disgraceth his head. 5 But every woman praying or proph-

esying with her head not covered disgraceth her head: for it is all one as if she were shaven. 6 For if a woman be not covered, let her be shorn. But if it be a shame to a woman to be shorn or made bald, let her cover her head.

Two things that are very important to notice in this verse are that Paul's concern is the public ministry (wow!)

Paul is talking about believers gathering (the church) in public assembly. In order to properly function in that role a woman (female pastor) and a man male pastor should be dressed properly. The male no covering on his head (that is dishonorable to the woman—a covering on her head, that is honorable.)

A veil in the Old Testament was a symbol of holiness and headship. It is central to understand that according to Paul, women and men were free to exercise ministry. Both could pray and prophecy. Either gender could do that, but it was crucial how they did it. This passage makes that emphasis. They must do it in different ways. The male as a man, the female as a woman.

Why must a woman wear a veil on her head? For three reasons:

1. Holiness
2. Angels
3. Authority

1). A woman in 1st century Corinth in public without a head covering was considered an idolater, witch, or a temple prostitute. Therefore, any woman appearing on the streets opened herself up for suspicion that she was available to any man who wanted to pay the price. Therefore, she was disqualified from ministering the WORD in a public assembly.

2). This verse in somewhat obscure, but what we know is that angels were present at creation, and thus understand the principle of headship. Evidently God's heavenly host were present at the meeting as angels are present in every believer's life (Eph. 3:10)

"To the intent that now unto the principalities and powers in heavenly places might be known by the church the manifold wisdom of God, according to the eternal purpose which he purposed in Christ Jesus our Lord."

and it would be a disgrace not to honor your head in the presence of angels.

3). Authority to do what, Paul? Certainly it has already been mentioned, it is what the whole passage is about (public ministry)—a women ministering the WORD in public.

So in conclusion,

The head or headship doesn't mean that the husband have the upper hand or the wife has no rights or she is a second class citizen, put in another way headship is an issue of order by God to love his wife like Christ loved the church to protect her, care for her and the like. Therefore, men do not lose your head over Headship (**Public Library Ray Stedman**)

Far from a dictatorship perspective where one human yokes another human against his or her will, God prefers men and women to work in harmony, not repulsed by His commandments.

Romans 12:2 (KJV)

And be not conformed to this world: but be ye transformed by the renewing of your mind, that ye may prove what is that good, and acceptable, and perfect, will of God.

Men of the Light, men who claim to know God, men in the church have embraced secular ideology with respect to women preaching and have attempted to justify it by Paul's words, which they intentionally read by the law and not by the spirit, adversely bringing a schism in the body.

Chapter 14

IS THERE A SCHISM IN THE BODY?

God is speaking to the apostle Paul in a very sensitive, poetic form about spiritual gifts in the church.

When God calls a pastor he/she must have the gift to speak publicly what the Spirit says to the church in order to have a healthy, well-balanced ministry. Additionally, by faith they must live out what they preach.

The question at bar is, Is there a schism in the body? The answer is *yes*.

1 Corinthians 12:12-28

12For as the body is one, and hath many members, and all the members of that one body, being many, are one body: so also is Christ.

13For by one Spirit are we all baptized into one body, whether we be Jews or Gentiles, whether we be bond or free; and have been all made to drink into one Spirit.

14For the body is not one member, but many.

[15]If the foot shall say, Because I am not the hand, I am not of the body; is it therefore not of the body?

[16]And if the ear shall say, Because I am not the eye, I am not of the body; is it therefore not of the body?

[17]If the whole body were an eye, where were the hearing? If the whole were hearing, where were the smelling?

[18]But now hath God set the members every one of them in the body, as it hath pleased him.

[19]And if they were all one member, where were the body?

[20]But now are they many members, yet but one body.

[21]And the eye cannot say unto the hand, I have no need of thee: nor again the head to the feet, I have no need of you.

[22]Nay, much more those members of the body, which seem to be more feeble, are necessary:

[23]And those members of the body, which we think to be less honourable, upon these we bestow more abundant honour; and our uncomely parts have more abundant comeliness.

[24]For our comely parts have no need: but God hath tempered the body together, having given more abundant honour to that part which lacked.

[25]That there should be no schism in the body; but that the members should have the same care one for another.

[26]And whether one member suffer, all the members suffer with it; or one member be honoured, all the members rejoice with it.

[27]Now ye are the body of Christ, and members in particular.

[28]And God hath set some in the church, first apostles, secondarily prophets, thirdly teachers, after that miracles, then gifts of healings, helps, governments, diversities of tongues.

To answer whether or not there is a schism in the body we must first establish the woman's position in the body.

1 Corinthians 12:12

For as the body is one, and hath many members, and all the members of that one body, being many, are one body: so also is Christ.

Galatians 3:28

There is neither Jew nor Greek, slave nor free, male nor female, for you are all one in Christ Jesus.

Paul so eloquently states in 1 Corinthians 12:12 that we have many members, and all the members belong to one body and that body is Christ. He further explains the revelation in Galatians 3:28 that there should be no schism because there is neither male nor **female** for we are one in Christ.

When a male preacher calls women preaching a doctrine of demons from the synagogue of Satan, we certainly have a schism and a very dangerous one, primarily because he has no evidence of God visiting the alleged disobedience of a women with judgment.

This position is most dangerous because if the church is 40 percent male and 60 percent female, and the females believed the fallacy that women cannot preach, then 60 percent of God's revelation would be suppressed, which could possibly save 60 percent of His image, and Satan would have won the quantitative victory of souls won to Christ.

2 Peter 3:9

The Lord is not slow in keeping his promise, as some understand slowness. He is patient with you, not wanting anyone to perish, but everyone to come to repentance.

Certainly the eye (men preachers) have said to the hand (women preachers) I have no need of you.

Certainly those members of the body which we think less honorable (women preachers) we should bestow with more honor.

So yes, there is a schism in the body, and a house divided cannot stand. The only way this can be reconciled is through the one Spirit that we both drink out of, and that is the Lord.

Acts 10:34 (KJV)

Chapter 15

GOD IS NO RESPECTOR OF PERSON

Then Peter opened his mouth, and said, Of a truth I perceive that God is no respecter of persons.

A s mentioned earlier, God is not a respecter of persons. He is not sexist, racist, communist, homophobic, or the like, nor can He be. Because His divine nature was uncaused, we must logically conclude that it is changeless and timeless. And since He created space and humans, He must transcend anything that is physical in nature; therefore He does not participate in the thinking of mankind.

Because we have a fallen nature, people who do not have a keen ear for the Spirit of God often come under the odd predilection that God is like us.

Isaiah 55:8-11 (KJV)

For my thoughts are not your thoughts, neither are your ways my ways, saith the LORD. For as the heavens are higher than the earth, so are my ways higher than your ways, and my thoughts than your thoughts. For as the rain cometh down, and the snow from heaven, and returneth not thither, but watereth the earth, and maketh it bring forth and bud, that it may give seed to the sower, and bread to the eater: So shall my word be that goeth forth out of my mouth: it shall not return unto me void, but it shall accomplish that which I please, and it shall prosper in the thing whereto I sent it.

Chapter 16

THE VERDICT

VERDICT

Hebrew 13:8

Jesus Christ the same yesterday, and to day, and forever.

Malachi 3:6 (KJV)

For I am the LORD, I change not; therefore ye sons of Jacob are not consumed.

"We the jury find by preponderance of empirical evidence that almighty God, on the charge of count one in the named indictment, is NOT GUILTY. Moreover the jury by a brief overview of His nature and character to be holy, righteous, faithful, sinless, immutable, sovereign, loving, omniscient, omnipotent, omnipresent..."

Chapter 17

THERE IS A BALM IN GILEAD

Jeremiah 8:22

Is there no balm in Gilead? Is there no physician there? Why then is not the health of the daughter (women preachers) of my people recovered

The Holy Bible refers to Jeremiah the Prophet as "The Weeping Prophet." Jeremiah began his ministry sixty years after the great evangelical prophet Isaiah. Some of Jeremiah's contemporaries in the ministry were Daniel Habakkuk, Zephaniah, Ezekiel and of course the prophetess Huldah.

Jeremiah ministered at a time of great tribulation for Judah but he was always comforted that there was a Balm in Gilead.

Balm of Gilead was a type of Gum grown only in Israel that was said to have healing properties.

Jeremiah succinctly declared is there no balm in Gilead? Is there no physician there? Why then is there no recovery for the health of my daughters. (women preachers)

Recently I was speaking to one of the younger female ministers in the church, inquiring about her recent summer vacation she took in Virginia. I asked so how was trip, she replied "very grievous" I responded oh Pastor told us about the departure of your uncle, death is always grievous, even Christ cried at Lazarus grave. She replied, I loved my uncle dearly and I was sad to see him depart, but actually that wasn't the major part of my grief. I asked well what was it? She responded I was chosen to officiate at the funeral, they allowed me to do all of the background work, but as I approached the Pulpit a deacon stopped me and told me that I wasn't allowed to stand in Holy Ground (the Pulpit).

As I walked in the procession, I noticed that the men walked two by two and they allowed me to walk alone until a man from out of the crowd approached me and said. Don't fret sister I will walk with you.

Well needless to say my emotions took over my heart started to palpitate, my hands started to get cold and clammy and anxiety was the order of the moment. I kept saying to myself please don't let me walk up to this pulpit and get rejected, moments later the scripture in Job 3:25-26 met me face to face.

Job 3:25-26

²⁵For the thing which I greatly feared is come upon me, and that which I was afraid of is come unto me.
²⁶I was not in safety, neither had I rest, neither was I quiet; yet trouble came.

She then asked me this profound question with her face fraught with innocence.

HOW COME GOD CAN TRUST THE WOMAN TO CARRY THE LIVING WORD BUT SHE CAN'T BE TRUSTED TO PREACH THE WRITTEN WORD.

I responded, there's a Balm in Gilead. Jeremiah 8:22

Jesus was your type of Jeremiah in so far that He was the GREAT PHYSICIAN and when we confess Him as LORD, THE SPIRIT then begins to apply the balm to our souls.

Jesus came to restore Paradise that was lost. In the Garden prior to Adam sinning the type of sexism that this woman experienced was not even known to mankind. The emotional trauma, experienced by attempting to serve God and simultaneously experience degradation because of gender is a great illness that requires major surgery.

Today in this reading Almighty God has taken the gloves off and He has begun to perform surgery with the revelation of His word. It is the reception of His word that acts as a Balm in the hearts of believers and when a believer is "Committed to Truth" only then does the medicinal affects start to heal the hearts of the offender and the offended. In the words of Gwen Wilkins Freeman a mighty woman of God, after she read this manuscript she stated "I get it, I get it, it's so clear, it's so clear, it's been in front of my face the last 30 years I have been saved and I never received it truly there is a Balm in Gilead for the Daughters of God. I feel like I am healed of a sickness that I thought was incurable."

Yes God wants women and men of all walks of life to know that not only do they have a Biblical basis to preach but if they refuse the God ordained commission they are in sin according to **James 4:17.**

¹⁷Therefore to him that knoweth to do good, and doeth it not, to him it is sin.

No more shall a woman called to preach hide behind the pulpit and not walk in her God given authority. God never gave a woman a right to usurp authority over her husband or undermine his God given role and she naturally knows that, nor did God call man to treat his wife like a slave and he naturally knows that, it is sin for both. But like Miriam and the pantheon of other bold, holy women, God has called them to Preach.

Perfect love cast out all fear. Because satan is who he is (a skilled liar) he has caused opponents of women preaching to confuse categories when the subject of preaching takes place. Satan has deceived these thinkers into thinking that when a woman pastors a church she usurps his God given male attributes. Jesus clearly explained the office of a prophet or prophetess in Luke 4:16.

Luke 4:16

[18]The Spirit of the Lord is upon me, because he hath anointed me to preach the gospel to the poor; he hath sent me to heal the brokenhearted, to preach deliverance to the captives, and recovering of sight to the blind, to set at liberty them that are bruised,

1) Preach the Gospel
2) Heal the brokenhearted
3) Proclaim liberty to the captives
4) Give sight to the blind

Whenever a man's natural dominant attribute is threatened, it causes fear and this is the plan of satan and it has prevailed for centuries but as you can see, there is nothing threatening to a man's masculinity by preaching Christ, nothing threatening to man's masculinity by healing the brokenhearted, or proclaiming liberty to the captives.

Today in this reading of this 2008 Revelation from the Holy Spirit women of all walks of life and even different faith's should receive an instant healing. The healing doesn't come from the authors theology the healing comes from the fact that your calling at last can be Biblically defended which adversely should increase your faith conversely clearing your conscience and convicting your calling. I didn't say you wouldn't still experience nay sayers, gainsayers, and the like the old motif says, "The truth will be the truth if everyone denies it, and a lie will be a lie if everyone embraces it." Nevertheless when Almighty God confirms your position, Romans 8:31 becomes your Balm.

Romans 8:31

If God be for you, who can be against you.

Thank you Jesus I am healed.

Chapter 18

A HOUSE DIVIDED CANNOT STAND

Matthew 12:22-31

22 Then a demon-possessed man, who was blind and could not speak, was brought to Jesus. He healed the man so that he could both speak and see. 23 The crowd was amazed and asked, "Could it be that Jesus is the Son of David, the Messiah?"

24 But when the Pharisees heard about the miracle, they said, "No wonder he can cast out demons. He gets his power from Satan, the prince of demons."

25 Jesus knew their thoughts and replied, "Any kingdom divided by civil war is doomed. A town or family splintered by feuding will fall apart. 26 And if Satan is casting out Satan, he is divided and fighting against himself. His own kingdom will not survive. 27 And if I am empowered by Satan, what about your own exorcists? They cast out demons, too, so they will condemn you for what you have said. 28 But if I am casting out demons by the Spirit of God, then the Kingdom of God has arrived among you. 29 For who is powerful enough to enter the house of a strong man like Satan and plunder his goods? Only someone even stronger—someone who could tie him up and then plunder his house.

30 "Anyone who isn't with me opposes me, and anyone who isn't working with me is actually working against me.

31 "So I tell you, every sin and blasphemy can be forgiven—except blasphemy against the Holy Spirit, which will never be forgiven.

God declared in **Isaiah 53:1** that He would physically show His arm to Israel through the Messiah and He did. When Jesus performed His miracles He did not do them in Germany, Poland, Spain, Central America, Antarctica, and Africa He did them strictly in Israel.

Isaiah 53:1

[1]Who hath believed our report? and to whom is the arm of the LORD revealed?

What type of miracles did He do?

1) Raised the Dead (only God can do)
2) Forgave sin (only God can do)
3) Healed the blind (only God can do)
4) Demons worshipped Him (Demons submit to no one but GOD)
5) Walked on water (Only God can defy the laws of gravity)
6) He controlled the elements (only God can do)
7) He resurrected (only God can do)

Even with all that they saw, they asked the offensive question could this be (The Son of David) which was the expected Messiah.

Jesus defense was in 3 parts.

First, a kingdom, city, or family cannot continue to exist if it is divided against itself.

Second, when the followers of the Pharisees exorcised demons the Pharisees claimed it was by the power of God.

Third, the casting out of demons indicated that Jesus was from God. Nevertheless, they called him Beelzebub. Imagine that. You see the Gentiles never physically experienced Jesus and believed but the Jews physically saw it and did not believe.

That is why in **John 20:19-29**

Jesus Appears to His Disciples

19 That Sunday evening[a] the disciples were meeting behind locked doors because they were afraid of the Jewish leaders. Suddenly, Jesus was standing there among them! "Peace be with you," he said. 20 As he spoke, he showed them the wounds in his hands and his side. They were filled with joy when they saw the Lord! 21 Again he said, "Peace be with you. As the Father has sent me, so I am sending you." 22 Then he breathed on them and said, "Receive the Holy Spirit. 23 If you forgive anyone's sins, they are forgiven. If you do not forgive them, they are not forgiven."

Jesus Appears to Thomas

24 One of the twelve disciples, Thomas (nick-named the Twin) was not with the others when

Jesus came. 25 They told him, "We have seen the Lord!"

But he replied, "I won't believe it unless I see the nail wounds in his hands, put my fingers into them, and place my hand into the wound in his side."

26 Eight days later the disciples were together again, and this time Thomas was with them. The doors were locked; but suddenly, as before, Jesus was standing among them. "Peace be with you," he said. 27 Then he said to Thomas, "Put your finger here, and look at my hands. Put your hand into the wound in my side. Do not be faithless any longer. Believe!"

28 "My Lord and my God!" Thomas exclaimed.

29 Then Jesus told him, "You believe because you have seen me. Blessed are those who believe without seeing me."

Jesus told Thomas because thou hast seen me thou hast believed but blessed are they that have not seen, and yet believed. This was Jesus prophetically talking about the Gentile nation. It was not that the Jews could not believe, it it was that they would not believe.

I would be evil according to scripture **Romans 14:16** if I didn't appeal to the opponents of women preaching with love and gentleness, not because I have an ulterior motive like being politically correct or I have some sort of liberal ideology. On the contrary, I have very conservative, orthodox Biblical views that is why I believe that it is wrong and even sinful to bar genuinely gifted women from the ministry.

Romans 14:16

[16]Let not then your good be evil spoken of:
I do believe in essentials there is unity, on non-essentials there is liberty and in all things, there is love, but to silence an anointed gifted voice could only come from the god of this age 2nd **Corinthians 4:3-4.**

2nd **Corinthians 4:3-4.**

[3]But if our gospel be hid, it is hid to them that are lost:
[4]In whom the god of this world hath blinded the minds of them which believe not, lest the light of the glorious gospel of Christ, who is the image of God, should shine unto them.

Satan has caused us to believe in the conservative Christian circle that women are expected to live contently in the background, presumably to focus on domestic duties, because this is their humble God ordained place in life. It is a place of invisible service and of godly but quiet influence over children and home or perhaps over the church nursery, Sunday school class, or Women's Bible study.

Satan has taken words like headship, rule, submit and deceived opponents specifically men that women are manipulating roles when the Gospel is not gender based, and it has divided our kingdom, additionally has deceived the church into thinking that women are more easily deceived than men which is a flat out lie which can be proven by the statistical data of the Bureau of Prisons.

In the spirit of **Isaiah 1:18** let us come reason together through the scriptures. These are the last days and satan's time is short and he has come down with great wrath. It is crucial, central, germane, axiomatic that the church unite as a body. God is not the author of confusion. One of the examiners, Bonita Spearman stated after she read this manuscript it is so clear, even a child could understand this.

> *[18]Come now, and let us reason together, saith the LORD: though your sins be as scarlet, they shall be as white as snow; though they be red like crimson, they shall be as wool.*

Jesus said in **Matthew 18:1-5** that we must become like children (humble, dependent, and meek) this is the only way that the kingdom can survive.

> *[1]At the same time came the disciples unto Jesus, saying, Who is the greatest in the kingdom of heaven?*
> *[2]And Jesus called a little child unto him, and set him in the midst of them,*
> *[3]And said, Verily I say unto you, Except ye be converted, and become as little children, ye shall not enter into the kingdom of heaven.*
> *[4]Whosoever therefore shall humble himself as this little child, the same is greatest in the kingdom of heaven.*
> *[5]And whoso shall receive one such little child in my name receiveth me.*

Scripture say in **Matthew 24:14** that this Gospel will be preached in all the earth then the end will come.

> *[14]And this gospel of the kingdom shall be preached in all the world for a witness unto all nations; and then shall the end come.*

Clearly, the woman is the helpmate with this task and since the Gospel is not gender oriented, God has called the woman to preach.

May God as He stimulate, motivate, revelate His maid-servants to preach, and may He adversely unveil the hearts of her counterparts in the Kingdom of God. Let us fervently pray that the Spirit who inspired the scriptures illuminate our minds to what is in the text.

Chapter 19

GET YOUR PEDICURE READY

Romans 10:15 (KJV)

And how shall they preach, except they be sent? as it is written, How beautiful are the feet of them that preach the gospel of peace, and bring glad tidings of good things!

Joel 2:28 (KJV)

And it shall come to pass afterward, that I will pour out my spirit upon all flesh; and your sons and your daughters shall prophesy, your old men shall dream dreams, your young men shall see visions.

What is God saying in these two verses?

He is saying that it is a beautiful thing for a person to preach the gospel, and if it is accomplished through the Holy Spirit, it will be done without regard to race, gender, age, or social class.

Today, after reading this book, women are able to sanctify the Lord God in their hearts and be ready always to give an answer to every man that asks them a reason for their calling. You should have a clean, clear conscience that when others speak evil of you, they may be ashamed that they falsely accuse your good conversation in Christ.

Today women can walk boldly in their anointing and calling because of the revelation in this book. The letter kept you hiding behind the pulpit (not being able to give men a reason for your hope). It kept you afraid, paranoid, double-minded, and the like. But the Spirit gave you life. You know Bishop Jakes loosed you; now this book freed you. Whom the Son sets free is free indeed!

So ladies, get your pedicure ready. There is not a soul on this earth, no matter how crafty, that can debate this 2008 revelation from the HOLY SPIRT of GOD.

P.S.

In most letters when a person forgot to put something in the letter an omission, endearment and the like they put P.S. Then they begin to reveal their thoughts. In this chapter, P.S. doesn't just stand for (Post Script); it stands for (Paul Said)..............Put your seat belt on!

The Apple Doesn't Fall Far From the Tree
(The Superseding Indictment Can A Woman Pastor?)

Most recently while discussing this revelation with two men Robert McLaurin a Southern Baptist who happens to be my father and W.T. a devoted man of God and friend of the family, they both took an authoritative stance that super-seded Scripture which I coin as the Superseding Indictment. "A woman can preach; she cannot pastor a church."

What was telling was that neither man knew one another but their thinking was like-minded. Robert McLaurin quoted, "Yes, I believe a woman can preach" and prefaced Mary Magdalene to support his theory, but turned around one month later during a conversation and said I don't believe a woman can pastor a church but offered no scriptural basis for his assertion. W.T. was different from the onset of the inter-change he didn't believe in women preaching but later stated that a woman can preach, but she cannot pastor. I chuckled endearingly within myself because if you read Paul's saying as a literalist, scripture clearly says that, "Women shouldn't speak at all in the church," which led me to investigate the Apple and the Tree.

I coined this chapter the Apple and the Tree as a means of symbolism. The Apple refers to the New Testament English; the tree (root) refers to the New Testament Greek. Although these men offered no scriptural basis for their theology a very erudite Pastor, and friend of mine who Pastors a church in Colwyn, PA wisely offered scripture to buttress his position:

> 1 Timothy 3:1, 2
> *This is a true saying, if a man desires the office of a Bishop he desireth a good work. (2) A Bishop then must be blameless, the husband of one wife, vigilant, sober of good behavior, given to hospitality, apt to teach.*

> Titus 1:6
> *If a man be blameless, the husband of one wife, having faithful children not accused of dissipation or insubordination. (NKJV)*

At first blush when you read this scripture the discussion stops and the person arguing that a woman should pastor throws the towel in and concedes that ok you have a point, I come in agreement, but when you give scripture the "Acid Test," you will once again see "What God" clearly said. When giving scripture the acid test you go to another level not just line by line or pretext by pretext, put in another way, you go to the original text. Let's examine the tree.

Firstly, manuscript evidence for the New Testament is abundant. There are more than 5,000 existing copies many with NT books largely intact. Also there are pantheons of older translations of the NT into languages like Syriac, Coptic and Latin that has survived in thousands of manuscripts no work of antiquity even approaches the NT for its authenticity. To that end I looked up 1st Timothy 3:1 and Titus 1:6 in the Greek it is translated as (tis) which means any or anyone.

In verse two of the English version, it states, "the bishop must be the husband of one wife." In the original Greek text, it reads the underscored below:

Ei	tis	eimi	angegkEtos	heis	gunE	anEr
If	any	is	unimpeachable	of one	woman	man
					Wife	husband

1st Timothy 3:5 says in the English version, "if a man know not how to rule his household." The Greek says something slightly different:

Ei	de	tis
If	yet	anyone

So clearly it's not Minister Lamont's thinking or the three gentlemen aforementioned in the previous text opinion. It's the Word of God clearly seen in the Greek that refers to Bishops as anyone and the qualification to be man or woman. Not only is the thesis biblically sound, it is supported overwhelmingly in Romans 16:3, *"Greet Priscilla and Aquila, my helpers in Christ Jesus.*

Q. What is your personal occupation?

Q. Do you have any co-workers, co-laborers, or fellow workers?

Q. If yes, what makes them your co-workers, co-laborers, or fellow workers?

A. I would presume that your answer would be because we perform the same task or job description.

Q. What was Paul's occupation in Christ Jesus?
A. He was pastor over all churches.

Q. What was Priscilla's gender?
A. A woman

Q. Did Paul say greet just Aquila or Aquila and Priscilla, my fellow workers in Christ?

A. Scripture says Priscilla and Aquila.

Case closed. God said that Priscilla, a woman, was a **pastor**, and if you read the entire chapter of Romans 16, you will observe that Paul greeted 26 people in this chapter, 1/3 of whom were women.

P.S.

Scripture is clear. A woman can **pastor** a church!

Bibliography

Cloud, David., Fundamental Baptist Information Service, P.O. Box 610368, Port Huron, MI 48061, 866-295-4143, fbns@wayoflife.org;

Hanegraaff, Hank. Bible Answer Book, Volume I and II

McTernan, John and Bill Koenig,, Israel the Blessing or the Curse,

Mears, Henrietta.. What the Bible is all about.

Nelson Study Bible N.K.J.V.

New Ungers Bible Dictionary

Stedman, Ray. What is Headship.

Strobel, Lee. The Case for the Faith

Biography

Minister Lamont McLaurin is a multi gifted national motivational speaker, an ex police officer who currently works full time as a High School Theology teacher in Philadelphia, Pennsylvania and a part time Social Worker, additionally he is a mid level consultant for several Oil companies.

Lamont's upcoming books are entitled:

You will never know God is all you need until you realize that God is all you have.

And...

The revelatory... If the Jews are GOD's chosen people, Is GOD the first Racist?

A revelatory defense of GOD's position concerning the Jews.

Printed in the United States
220420BV00001B/225/P